ADVENTUROUS JOURNEY
FROM PEACE TO WAR,
INSURGENCY TO TERRORISM

Vijitha Yapa Publications
Unity Plaza, 2 Galle Road, Colombo 4, Sri Lanka
Tel: (94 11) 2556600 Fax: (94 11) 2816511
e-mail: vijiyapa@gmail.com
www.vijithayapa.com
www.srilankanbooks.com

ISBN 978-955-665-042-6

First Edition July 2009
Second Revised Edition February 2010

Printed by Tharanjee Prints, Sri Lanka

ADVENTUROUS JOURNEY
FROM PEACE TO WAR,
INSURGENCY
TO TERRORISM

by

General Cyril Ranatunga

VIJITHA YAPA
PUBLICATIONS
www.vijithayapa.com

Contents

Acknowledgements

The leaders of the country who I was associated with and served under — reflected in the book for their understanding and tolerance.

I am grateful to my friends who helped in many ways and to those who contributed articles, photographs etc. Brig. Daya Wijesekera (retd) for his assistance in collecting all available material including my handwritten notes and putting them together.

Prof. K.M. De Silva, Mr. Dushyantha Mendis and members of the staff of I.C.E.S. Kandy and Mrs. Amali Ellegalle Seneviratna formerly of I.C.E.S. Kandy for their assistance and commitment to make this a success

Miss Thiruni Kelagama for rewriting the book under the guidance of Prof. K.M. de Silva.

I am grateful to all my comrades of the Armed Forces and the Police who teamed up to make a cohesive formation to eradicate terrorism from our motherland. Their commitment and devotion have been appreciated and respected.

I thank many friends and well-wishers who did not want publicity or recognition for working in the interest and well being of the nation.

Most of all I am grateful to my family, Myrtle, Niran, Ranmalie, Rajind, Minal and the grandchildren especially Rawin.

The staff of Vijitha Yapa Publications for their valuable contribution in editing and publishing this book.

Foreword

This volume consists of the memoirs of a soldier coping with the tensions in the country during a crucial period in its affairs. It begins first of all with the early days of the army when it was merely a parade ground outfit, and then moves on to organising the first faltering steps in which the army was involved in the state's resistance to the first Janatha Vimukthi Peramuna (JVP) insurgency of 1971. Cyril Ranatunga played a key role, both in the resistance to the JVP, and then in the reconstruction that followed. The second phase in his memoirs begins with him leading the armed forces in organising the resistance to the Liberation Tigers of Tamil Eelam (LTTE) movement of the Tamil minority and their campaign against the Sri Lankan state. The chapters of this volume, which deal with the Vadamarachchi campaign, are a lively account of the army in action, and its triumphs in that struggle. The army led by Ranatunga were on the verge of even more significant victories such as the capture of the town of Jaffna when the Indian intervention saved the LTTE from further and more humiliating defeats. He had reorganised the army from this setback when it became time for him to leave on what he thought would be his return to civilian life. He embarked on a short stint of diplomatic life as his country's High Commissioner in Australia and then, as High Commissioner in the United Kingdom of Great Britain and Northern Ireland. After that period of service in the United Kingdom was over, it was civilian life again.

Before his brief period of service in the diplomatic field began he had served as the civilian head of the reconstruction and expansion of the island's airport at Katunayake. He enjoyed this work very much indeed.

After completing the diplomatic service in the United Kingdom he retired to civilian life in his house in the town of Mawanella. He had a garden and about 13 acres of productive land in which he had time to live the life of a rather prosperous agriculturalist. From Mawanella he led the re-organization of life at the scenic Kadugannawa Pass where a large mass of small shops hindered the view of the land beyond the pass. It was civilian service done with great tact and skill.

As this volume would show he had two generations of life in the Sri Lanka Army—a unique record that is worth talking about. His memoirs are a historical source of great value to those who study contemporary Sri Lanka.

K.M. de Silva

Preface

The war to liberate every inch of our island is over; the powerful LTTE war machinery has been destroyed and the leaders are dead. The nation is grateful to the Security Forces and greatly appreciate their success. The greatest human hostage crisis in the world has ended and the civilians under the control of the LTTE have been freed.

In 2009, though there was pressure from the West and also from South India, there were no air drops of food. This is quite in contrast to what I faced when our troops had cornered the LTTE during Operation Liberation in Vadamarachchi in 1987.

Retirement, many say, is the second lease of life one receives after years of challenging work. In my case, I was gifted with the most valuable gift of all: that of **time**, to enjoy all that I had missed during my entire public service, ranging over 43 years – a life of hardship, danger and excitement. A life I have never to this day regretted.

It was only following retirement that I came back to my ancestral property, which was left for me by my parents in Mawanella, called *Erabudhupela Estate* in which I live today with Myrtle. My two sons with their families visit us whenever they find the time to get away from Colombo. This piece of land, which I find simply wonderful, is tucked away just two miles off the main Colombo–Kandy Road. It is on this piece of land that I was able to take a well-deserved and as most say, a hard-earned break from the military life that I had become accustomed to, and try my hand at farming. It would be safe to say that at present, I am one happy farmer!

In spite of being a person solely committed to the military, agriculture has always been my hobby and the land I own has given me the wonderful opportunity to practice it. I cultivate the paddy fields that feed me. I grow all varieties of bananas. My dairy farm with six

x

healthy cows provides me with milk. The manure and the leaves of the 'albizia' trees is good fertilizer for the vegetables and the paddy. What is more important is perhaps the fact that the 'bio-gas' plant provides the 'fuel' for cooking. Fruit trees such as guavas and mangoes, and the all purpose 'beli' grow quite well. I also grow pepper, coconuts and rubber. A walk through my estate will not refresh any tired soul, but will open one's eyes to the simple wonders of nature and agriculture, and will enable one to envisage the happiness which is an immeasurable part of the life I lead today.

Needless to say, I am satisfied with the results. And more satisfied with the quiet life I lead. It was on one such day that I was prompted to write the story of my life; to be more precise, to record in writing, the military history that I had been part of. My initial reaction was hesitation. It seemed too daunting a task. However, despite my indecisiveness, I felt that maybe I should endeavour to chronicle my life story and put into writing what I had to say: to speak of the history I had watched unravelling in front of my own eyes. I wish to express my gratitude to Thiruni Kelagama who helped to put the narrative in a presentable form.

And once I started, I realized that I indeed had so much to say… For the first time, I was putting years of military action and military thoughts into words. This book is the final result – it is here that I finally present the **Cyril Ranatunga Story**. A story which I hope would thereby justify my making valid claims on behalf of the country that I had dedicated my entire life to the country I call my own.

Cyril Ranatunga

Early Years

I was born on 19 February 1930 to a family of six children; three brothers, two sisters and myself. My brothers and I were all educated at St. Sylvester's College, one of the leading schools in the district and right in the heart of the historic town of Kandy. We were born in the village of Bakmeedeniya, near Kegalle where my father was living at the time. My elder brother George, who is no longer living, retired as a colonel from the army. The other brothers Bertie and Chandra are also professionals: one a licensed surveyor and the other practising law in the Kegalle Bar respectively. Chandra was also Deputy Minister of Housing and Construction under President Ranasinghe Premadasa (1990-1994). One of my sisters lives in the land adjoining mine in Mawanella, while the other lives in Colombo.

The years 1939-1945 were the years of World War II, when Great Britain was in the vanguard of the struggle to defeat Nazi Germany and later, Japan. It was in this background that I was attending school, in the early years of 1940.

Sri Lanka, like all other countries under British rule, was involved in World War II. It was a familiar sight to see soldiers from almost all the countries in the British Empire stationed in barracks throughout the country. Young men enlisted, although most, if not all, were unaware of the horrors of war. The enthusiasm was largely due to their desire to 'see the world' particularly by joining the Navy. Some joined the British units and served remarkably well, especially in the Middle Eastern theatre. Colombo experienced a Japanese bombing raid in April 1942 and many in Colombo moved up to the interior, and this resulted in the schools in Colombo being moved up country. Subsequently, Kandy became a hive of military activity as the headquarters of Lord Louis Mountbatten, Commander of the South East Asia Command, was established in the spacious and beautiful Royal Botanical Gardens at Peradeniya.

2

This 'military' environment would certainly have influenced any youth at the time to decide on a professional military career, and I was no exception. I was duly impressed by the smartly turned out officers and soldiers moving around in varied colourful uniforms of their countries in assorted types of vehicles. There were also numerous military units consisting of the huge, turbaned, bearded Sikhs, the Punjabis, Marathas, the small-made but smart Gurkha troops in their special hats wearing the unmistakable Kukri, and African troops, besides British troops who were garrisoned in Kandy and the neighbouring areas. Half track 'Bren' gun carriers were a special attraction at the time to any youth, as it was for me. These officers and soldiers also played cricket, rugby and football with local teams, which helped develop a better understanding and rapport with the local people.

My parents bought a house in Kandy Town for two simple, nevertheless important, reasons. First, Mawanella, where my family had their ancestral home, was little more than a village with the commercial centre confined mainly to a small town on either side of the main Colombo-Kandy Road, today known as the A-1 Road. It only provided the basic facilities as a centre of the Tea and Rubber plantations, largely managed by the British planters. Secondly, the schools were village schools offering no facilities for education in English. They also did not have extracurricular activities such as sports. These restricted education facilities were not quite sufficient to provide opportunities to compete successfully in life. My father insisted that his children be able to participate fully in extracurricular activities to attain a more rounded character. He was also adamant that we received the best that education had to offer. He selected St. Anthony's College in Kandy, which was the premier Roman Catholic school in the Kandy District, with ample opportunities to participate in school activities. The section of St. Anthony's College, which I attended, was later set up as a separate school, presently renamed St. Sylvester's College.

As a schoolboy, I captained the College hockey and athletic teams, while studying for the Senior School Certificate exam. These all round performances earned me the position of Head Prefect and the Gold Medal for Best All Round Student in 1949.

Joining the Army

With the colonial system drawing to a close and with the decline of the British Empire, Sri Lanka gained Independence a few months after India. Sri Lanka (then Ceylon until 22 May 1972) was granted Independence on 4 February 1948 and with the establishment of the Regular army on 10 October 1949, officer cadets vacancies were advertised in the newspapers and in the government gazette. After the preliminary interview, the final interview was before the three service commanders, all of whom were British officers. As a young man, the military and the uniform fascinated me immensely. Hence, I had no hesitation about applying for a vacancy. I was selected as an officer cadet in April 1950. This, as I fondly recollect, was the start of my life in the army.

The urgent need at the time was to establish officer training to replace the British officers. The UK was the obvious choice for more advanced officers' training. In the UK, the officer cadets were trained at the Officer Cadet School at Mons, Aldershot, and thereafter at the Royal Military Academy (RMA) at Sandhurst. Each year at least four officer cadets were sent for training to RMA and on their return were posted to regiments. They were invariably assigned to train recruits at the Army Recruit Training Depot (ARTD), Diyatalawa, as the army demanded more soldiers to raise regiments.

My RMA batch consisted of nearly 1,500 cadets: junior, intermediate and senior intakes included. I was assigned Marne Company, which had about 207 students including those from Saudi Arabia, Malta, Burma (Myanmar), Fiji, Jordan and Malaysia. There were six cadets from Ceylon (Sri Lanka). My Company Commanders were Majors Pritchard and Brooke Smith. The platoon commanders of the Company were Pat Porteous, Sanderson and Blundell-Brown. Pat Porteous later went on to win the Victoria Cross, the highest honour awarded for the display of valour on the field. Many cadets from

Ceylon had a reasonably good working knowledge of English and were also able to participate in sports activities, though a few found the English language somewhat challenging.

At RMA, the commissioning parade was known as the 'Sovereigns' Parade. At the ceremony the cadets go in procession up the steps of the old college and the doors open. When all the passing out cadets go through, followed by the adjutant on horseback, the doors close. The moment that happens you are commissioned. Generally, the sovereign himself will witness the parade, though on occasion he would be represented by a member of the royal family.

The commissioning parade for my batch unfortunately coincided with the death of the Sovereign: King George VI. For the first time in the long history of RMA – of over two hundred years – the parade had to be cancelled. My batch, therefore, was the first to be commissioned by Her Majesty Queen Elizabeth II, though this was a pure formality, without any ceremony. Fifty years later, that event was commemorated in the UK by those who belonged to that batch, together with their families. Some no longer amongst the living were represented by their wives or by a member of their family. This is an aspect of the proud tradition of comradeship which was encouraged in the British Army.

RMA training was followed by a course in jungle warfare in Malaysia conducted at Far East Land Forces (FARELF) by British Jungle Warfare Instructors who had trained officers and soldiers during World War II. The course was conducted at the Jungle Training School in Kota Tingi in Johore Baru. Its aim was to train officers in anti-bandit operations, to meet the threat of bandits who were spread out in the jungles of Malaysia, foraging from the neighbouring villages for their livelihood and raiding governmental organizations.

Jungle Warfare School was surrounded by jungle with firing ranges to practice at opportunity targets that appear suddenly through scrub and disappear. This is to test and improve your response whilst patrolling in bandit country and the test is to obtain maximum score with ten rounds of ammunition. Many innovative methods of training were adopted. A battalion of Gurkha Rifles were used for demonstration and was also used to provide security to the school.

We had two field exercises. However, precautions were necessary at every stage. Before we went into the jungle, we were expected to sign a document indicating that we were going voluntarily as the organizers did not want to take a chance with the foreign students. The patrols were to take on known bandit camps. On reaching the first camp we found it had been abandoned a few days earlier. The second camp was live but the bandits were out. What we did, therefore, was stay in ambush for 24 hours and thereby destroyed the utility items found in the camp. The first time we were out for four days. The second time we were out for six days.

They were well-planned patrols of six or seven officers who went into the jungle on a grid bearing. We had to hack our way through the jungle and the worst was the Baluka grass. It grew over our heads and the only means of travel was with the aid of a compass bearing. Our map reading and compass bearing as a result had to be excellent. One member in the group was supposed to hold the compass and say, "Keep moving, keep left, keep a little more to the left...!" The rest of the patrol follow suit. Any deviation at the start and the result could be reaching a destination that maybe a mile away from your original target!

The only air support we received was the food drops. These had been planned prior to our departure and we had been informed of them before the patrol started. We were told that on a particular date, there would be an air drop at a specified place. There was no room for inactivity. We had to follow the map and reach the destination to clear the place for the air drop. Even then, we were not supposed to anticipate a food drop; we had to send smoke signals for the aircraft to drop the food. The first food drop we got was dog food! All we could do was burying it and forget all thoughts about food! The second drop however was fine, and lasted us for maybe three days.

This training proved to be very helpful during the long years of service later in my career. After receiving a training of nearly 24 months I was commissioned as a Second Lieutenant and posted to the Ceylon Light Infantry, the oldest and the 'core' regiment of the future Sri Lankan Army. My career had officially begun.

The 1953 'hartal' was engineered by Marxist parties as a non–violent demonstration and protest against the increment in the price of rice. It began as a peaceful demonstration, but it did not remain so. Soon the protest became unruly and violent, resulting in serious damage to government property and disruption of law and order. It was also the first occasion after Sri Lanka gained independence in 1948, when troops were deployed with instructions to use live ammunition to disperse protestors. Although not widespread and in terms of violence hardly close to what was to be part of our experience later, the 'hartal' showed the critical need for a unit with adequate mobility and flexibility to be deployed whenever and wherever speed was essential. This ensured the birth of the Ceylon Armoured Corps in 1955.

1ˢᵗ Recce Regiment

The 1ˢᵗ Recce Regiment was raised on 10ᵗʰ October 1955. The expansion was made with batches of recruits trained from December 1956 to December 1957. Vacancies for officers in the rank of Lieutenant in the new regiment were advertised in Army Orders. It was difficult for many to change regiments due to affiliations, friends and comrades, but I and some others who were like minded, applied with the sole intention of seeking a new way of life. Lieutenant S.D.N. Hapugalle, an officer in the Ceylon Electrical and Mechanical Engineers and myself from the Ceylon Light Infantry (CLI) were selected as the first officers of the newly formed regiment. At this point it may be helpful to the reader if I introduce the component units of the Army.

Usually an armoured corps troop comprises of one officer and thirty men. An officer with three sections makes up a troop, commanded by a troop leader who is usually a lieutenant or sergeant. In the Armoured Corps, a troop consists of many tanks and armoured cars.

We started the Armoured Corps with Ferret scout cars, Daimler armoured cars and Saladin armoured cars. One was usually expected to have four such vehicles in a troop. Three troops make a squadron. A squadron is commanded by a major and usually three squadrons with a headquarters squadron make a regiment.

Three regiments were usually needed to form a brigade. A brigade is formed with the amalgamation of regiments of armour, artillery, engineers and infantry. There were always three brigades to a division. What we have in the Sri Lanka Army is a number of brigades, some of them in combination making a division of all arms [i.e. armour, artillery, engineers and infantry], thus making the combined total sufficient for deployment in Sri Lanka.

Our Regiment was called a reconnaissance regiment — we were to be the eyes and ears of the army. A reconnaissance regiment is geared to move fast to carry out its functions. Small vehicles such as the Ferret scout cars went fairly fast to reconnoitre and pass on information. It is also a well-known fact that reconnaissance regiments are part and parcel of any large army.

The regiment we raised however was not purely for reconnaissance. As time progressed, its functions became much more complex and finally ended up as an Armoured Corps.

The vacancies for other ranks were also advertised and we were able to select the best available for the army, which then numbered a mere couple of thousands. At this time, over fifty years ago, soldiers enlisted not for want of an occupation but for the simple reason of being a soldier. Most, if not all of them, were fluent in English and life was also easy as in the villages from where they came. Most of the other ranks came from the Ceylon Light Infantry (CLI), the 'core' which provided for the expansion of the army incessantly. Today the attitude in the selection of men to new regiments is different and more complicated as Commanding Officers are reluctant to send the 'best,' due to the armed conflict with the LTTE. The best men are always in demand at all levels in combat situations. It is more likely that units would rather send out the average men instead of the best, unlike in the days gone by.

The motto of my new squadron was 'Whither the Fates Call' – the same as that of the Queen's Dragoon Guards. The first element of the squadron was established after an all night *pirith* ceremony at Echelon Barracks, Colombo, in the very heart of the island's capital, Fort, Colombo. Life at Echelon Barracks was neither comfortable nor pleasant with differences of opinion being aired incessantly, with the very interfering but likeable and helpful Camp Commandant, Captain Van Twest. A former British Army soldier, he was indeed huge, very ferocious in appearance and a stickler for discipline. Echelon Barracks was built by the British Army to accommodate the army and the navy. The name Echelon was derived as the buildings were arranged 'in echelon' to enable the sea breeze to blow through. British medical opinion at the time believed that good air circulation would reduce the sick rate of the British troops who were not acclimatized to the tropical climate. The barracks were part of the former Fort built by the Portuguese in the 16th Century, which the Dutch improved to withstand the cannon and heavy artillery at the time. The British in turn improved on this when they captured it from the Dutch on 16 February 1796. These barracks were demolished after independence, and the space so created now houses the Hotel Continental, the Hotel Galadari, the Central Bank Building and the Twin Towers, the highest building in our country. Remnants of the old Dutch Hospital still stand, but has now become of historical value as it houses Dutch archaeological items.

I believed that this location was highly unsuitable for raising a mechanized unit. Neither was it suitable for the training of officers and troops in their new equipment. As a result of this dissatisfaction, in 1956 the squadron was moved to Ridiyagama, about 150 miles south of Colombo with a better training ground – with vast open spaces more suited to the training. Ridiyagama was an outback, besides the reservoir, surrounded by mostly scrub jungle with vicious thorns and rugged terrain in the deep south of the island. Ridiyagama offered one immeasurable advantage: training could be conducted for the troops away from public scrutiny.

The complex we occupied formerly belonged to the Department of Agriculture, and had been set up for the Agricultural Corps raised by Prime Minister. D.S. Senanayake during the early years after Independence. The buildings were provided with the basic facilities: running water and electricity. Most of the dormitories were half-walled with good ventilation, and provided the soldiers the benefit of the cool breeze blowing across the huge Ridiyagama Reservoir (this camp was abandoned after the Agriculture Corps was disbanded). After a very long drive from Colombo, a few of the 'advance party' arrived in our new camp and were soon busy making preparations for the rest to follow.

We entered through huge gaps between the broken and dilapidated barbed wire which was supposed to be a perimeter fence. It did not even prevent the stray cattle getting in and settling down in the corridors of the buildings. The entire place appeared desolate, especially after the busy and congested atmosphere at Echelon Barracks. The first problem was not long in coming. Although we had brought with us the 'dry' rations, we needed 'fresh' rations for our meals. This we could not have until the arrival of the 'main' body which was expected only after another two days. But we had not run out of luck. I fortunately had with me the money from the sale of my dearest possession, the 'Indian' motorbike. This money was used to purchase fresh rations for two days for the advance party until the main body of troops arrived. I have still to claim for reimbursement of this 'soft' loan!

The troops settled down very fast in spite of the broken eggs provided by the contractor in lieu of meat. This means of providing eggs as a substitute was a convenient means for the contractor to make the maximum profit as it was cheaper than meat. The other common denominators in the menu were either *parippu* (dhal) or *wattakka* (pumpkin)! These were prepared in numerous ways, but if a vote was to be taken for preferences, I am convinced that *parippu* would have won the day with a huge majority! So, our cuisine comprised of *parippu* and rice, rice and *parippu*... The only mode of communication we had with Headquarters in Colombo was the HF 19 radio set up with improvised bamboo aerials working on morse.

Everything we encountered was a challenge and this was met with a spirit of adventure and high morale.

Amidst the daily challenges that we faced together as a troop, we set about the training schedules, basic as well as advanced and specialist training peculiar to the army, with enthusiasm. Maximum priority was provided for training and creating an *esprit de corps* for the future armoured regiments. Since we were still young, we were imbued with a sense of pride which enabled us to establish a new regiment.

The typical daily routine began with 'bed tea' at 0615 hours. Bed tea is a remnant dating back to the British speciality of having tea in bed. However, although known as bed tea amongst soldiers, it was hardly tea in bed! It was, in reality, queuing up at the kitchen door with an aluminium mug to obtain a cup of tea which was poured from a huge jug or kettle by the Mess orderly. It tasted more of powdered milk than tea! What is common in Mess tea is that wherever prepared, the taste remains more or less the same. Perhaps it is the water that is always on the boil! The first period of drill lasted until about 0800 hours. This may sound very early, but there were good reasons to adopt this schedule. First, it gave us an extra two hours of training and the opportunity to avoid the fierce sun between 1200 and 1500 hours. The morning session after breakfast ended at 1300 hours. After lunch, 'rest' was made compulsory. It was also time to attend to what was known as personal administration – cleaning boots and personal kit – or 'indoor economy.' The hot afternoons provided the time for instructors to prepare for the next training day. This was followed by indoor classes in weaponry, followed by physical training and sports until dusk. The technical trainees usually arrived for late lunch, but joined with the others for sports. As the training progressed, all trainees had the opportunity to learn as well as conduct classes on a variety of military subjects. They included, other than drill, driver training, gunnery, radio and assault trooper training. Instructional classes were conducted by officers of other units, and Captains M.W. Weerasinghe of the Mechanical Engineer and Noel Jobsz of the Signals Regiment were specialists in their fields and their instruction was invaluable. Due to this practice, young instructors and NCO's had the opportunity of gaining confidence of the majority of the troops who were fascinated by the innovative ideas used for methods of instruction.

I was also personally interested in shooting from my early days as a young officer. In Ridiyagama we constructed a 50-metre firing range. We used a .22 range for purposes of training and held inter-troop competitions in .22 firing. It is easy to have a practice range within a confined area thus making it possible to even have indoor .22 ranges.

Though the .22 was used to practice shooting, it is very accurate and categorized as small arms. There is even a .22 Olympic competition. The .303 is a basic weapon with a bigger calibre. This was used by all in the forces and in the police as well. The .303 was the personal weapon of every soldier. I was extremely enthusiastic about rifle shooting and I made sure that I carried my rifle during operations and of course, everywhere I went. I was confident that I could take on anybody. Now, the .303 is done away with and the soldiers carry with them a SLR and other weapons. I would maintain that even with the availability of automatic rifles, the .303 can still hold its own in the field.

We drove to Diyatalawa for .303 firing in the two ranges and field firing with the two pounder guns of the armoured cars. Troops enjoyed the few days spent in Diyatalawa and the firing practices.

Both Myrtle and I were members of the Negombo Rifle Club which was open to members on one Sunday of each month for competitions and practise firing. It was a relaxed day with other members who were friendly and very enthusiastic.

Another outing we looked forward to was the annual rifle meet conducted by the navy in Trincomalee.

At Ridiyagama, we were able to encourage weapon handling and accurate shooting, which resulted in producing outstanding marksmen, who in turn vied to find a place in the regimental team. The outcome was our ability to take on the oldest and more experienced units of the army – the 1 CLI and 2(v) CLI, both reputed teams in competition. I am proud to state our regiment carried away most of the trophies in the annual Inter-Unit Rifle meet. We also participated in the Ceylon Rifle Association meets. The most coveted trophy, the Governor's Cup, was won by our regiment. It involved a six-mile march in full battle order carrying rifle and ammunition. The target appears after 90 minutes from the start of your march and disappears after 50 seconds. That was the manner in which the signal to run 100 yards to the next firing point was given. This process continues until we reach the last firing point at 100 yards.

Everyone from the officer commanding to the most junior trooper participated in sports every evening on the rough and dirt of the available playing field. Popular games such as hockey, football, volleyball, 'soft' ball cricket and basketball were played vigorously and the matches were keenly contested. Within a few months, having meals, playing and working together ensured that we were a cohesive unit and everyone shouldered responsibility and heaved together. Yes, those were indeed good times amongst a wonderful lot of men...

I still reminisce how we worked for hours and days on end with the new recruits, to build a healthy *esprit de corps,* and a tradition worthy of emulation. Our squadron consisted of three officers including the commanding officer. Private Siripala had enlisted in spite of the fact that his civil status was inappropriate to enlist as a soldier. The basic requirement then for enlistment was that all recruits should be bachelors in their civil status. Siripala was however married but had not declared so in the application for enlistment, in his staunch determination to enlist. However, those were the days when the army checked out every detail regarding the civil life of their recruits including that of their grandparents. It is unfortunate that this practice was abandoned some years ago due to the pressures of recruitment, whilst introducing the politicians' 'chit' as a powerful factor in the selection of officers and recruits; these have had their own ill-effects on the service. The police check brought out the truth and Private Siripala had to face the ordeal of being marched up by then Sergeant Jayanetti – later commissioned as a Quarter Master – to the commanding officer who was Lieutenant Colonel Attygalle. The Colonel was not amused by Siripala's explanation and spoke his piece, but those who knew the Colonel were certain Siripala would get off the hook, which he did. Lt. Col. and later General Attygalle understood the soldier and the demands of society. He could give the most frightening tongue lashing, but if told the truth, would never let down a soldier.

The professional grading of soldiers was categorized as One, Two and Three stars. The soldiers were eligible for such grades only upon recommendation by the officer commanding (an officer who commands the sub-unit; a squadron etc.) and by the commanding officer (an officer who commands a battalion and regiment). The first 'star' was awarded after six months of service. Thereafter, it was required that they be tested for their professional skills for the second and third stars in weapons, map reading, drill signals etc, and only then were they recommended.

The armoured vehicles available to the new regiment were the Armoured Personnel Carriers (APC's) used by the British Army of World War II vintage. They served two important functions at the time. The first was the ability to move with speed to any location where and when they were required, and the ability to support the infantry. They were also fitted with a machine gun with a 360 degree traverse.

Secondly, perhaps the most important and valuable function was that they could be helpful in a show of force amongst unruly crowds by their mere presence. We by then possessed two turreted (Mk. II) and four unturreted (Mk. I) Ferret Scout Cars. In 1956 more MK II turreted FSC's arrived and needless to say boosted the morale of our regiment. At a latter stage, Daimler armoured cars reconditioned in the UK were brought down, which equipped the armoured corps. These vehicles were a familiar sight which created great interest in the regiment enabling it to attract some of the best soldiers and officers into the unit. They were in service until the 1980s.

As the commanding officer of the regiment, these vehicles were at my disposal when the Prime Minister appointed me as Coordinating Officer of Kegalle District during the JVP uprising in April 1971. I made due use of them and took the opportunity to indulge in test firing the guns on to the Bible Rock off Mawanella. This certainly drove fear into the JVP insurgent ranks and proved to be a major reason for their abandoning their Kegalle stronghold.

The reconnaissance troop also consisted of motorcycle combinations. Working on these combinations helped improve teamwork where soldiers learnt what could be achieved by working together as a team. As a motorcycle enthusiast myself, I quickly took to them. There were enough spills and thrills during the training sessions on the combinations, with many enthusiastic volunteer riders. There was Private Sirisena, a talented boxer who had joined from the 1 Field Engineers. He was found hanging on to some branches with his hands while trying to stop the motorbike which was running without brakes! There was ample space to learn how the combinations performed and we were able to participate in the 1956 Army Tattoo, the first ever to be held by the army after independence. After hours of practice riding and manoeuvring the bikes in the dirt tracks in the scorching heat of Ridiyagama, we could perform considerably well, most often on one wheel, carrying the combination in the air. This prompted us to improve and remodel the performance so that the wheel could be removed and then fitted whilst riding. This novel performance was appreciated by many who witnessed the Army Tattoo in 1956. The motorcycle combinations continued to be used until the 'Tattoo' had to be put on hold unfortunately in the beginning of the 1980s due to ongoing armed conflict which was escalating in a startling manner. The 'core' of the armoured corps had its origins with dedicated officers and soldiers from the WW II era. This regiment still owes a debt to the efforts of two unforgettable personalities, Captain & (QM) Ellis Martenstyn and Gordon Ingram. The two stood out in their technical knowledge and were the real 'mechanics' who shouldered the technical responsibilities. Captain Bob Evetts, a former Assistant Provost Marshal in the British Army during WW II served in the capacity of Motor Transport Sergeant.

By the end of 1956, the squadron had expanded to seven officers and 160 other ranks. In 1957 the troops were moved to Rock House, Mutwal, the former World War II site of the British Coast Artillery. The Rock House in Mutwal was the location for a complex of very heavy coastal artillery guns. They were mounted on emplacements built out of absolute concrete. There were rooms under the gun emplacements and the ammunition came up from there. The guns, which were really meant to fire at ships, could be moved in certain directions and elevated to give range. We moved in there as the Sri Lankan Artillery had no pressing use for those guns. Subsequently, some of the guns were auctioned by the army.

It was at this stage that I was selected for training which was to be conducted in Bovington, UK, in 1957 as the Regimental Signals Officer of the newly raised regiment. The only means of travel to the United Kingdom at that time was by ship and I travelled in the P&O liner 'Orantes.' It was there that I met a young lady, Ms. Myrtle Sumanasekera. The journey took three weeks and by the time we had reached the UK, romance had blossomed and fate deemed that we were to be married. This was successfully done by the registrar in Kensington, on 27 December 1957. The time that ensued involved a lot of travelling to London from Bovington at the first available opportunity and naturally there was never a dull moment!

The days recounted so far were pleasant while also being stimulating and challenging. However, the shadow which engulfs Sri Lanka even today, cast its first dark light at that time, and the use of violence by communal elements and the counter use of the armed forces to quell such disturbances ensued. This commenced in the late 1950s.

The 1958 communal riots required the regiment to engage in the maintenance of law and order in Ampara. In that year riots commenced in Ampara with the murder of Mr. D.A. Seneviratne, the Mayor of Nuwara Eliya, in Eravur. At that time, I was heavily involved in maintaining peace.

Meanwhile, my wife and I had been on a private trip to Kataragama and on our return I declared to Myrtle: "Give me anything in the world, I am not going to get up till late tomorrow!" Fate decided otherwise. It was no coincidence when at 3:00 a.m. there was an urgent knock on my door. Two young officers informed me, "The commanding officer is waiting for you to arrive at Rock House, and all squadron vehicles are ready to move to Ampara." By this time, Myrtle had become used to my way of life; she did not protest as I quickly rushed away...

After D.A. Seneviratne was killed in Eravur, the Gal Oya colonization scheme workers could not be silenced. Infuriated, they approached with their bulldozers to kill the Tamils. They wanted revenge. Fortunately, on my way to Ampara I was able to catch a glimpse of the oncoming convoy. I immediately stopped them at a distance and demanded to know where they were heading. The reply to my question was startling: "We are going to teach them a lesson!"

Having no other choice, I ordered the immediate dispersal of the crowds. But that was not the end. On my way from Eravur to Ampara I was shot at and got some pellets on me. One soldier was critically hurt. The significance of the incident lies in the fact that it was perhaps the very first time the army had to encounter an experience of being fired at by civilians.

In 1957, I set out to Trincomalee because the 'anti sri campaign' organized by the Federal Party had gotten underway at that time. This campaign was organized by the foremost Tamil party at the time in the country, against the new system of allocating letters and numbers in the registration of vehicles; the Federal Party objected to the use of the Sinhala letter 'Sri,' saying it was discriminatory against the Tamils. Amongst the orders I received, one was specific in its nature – I was asked not to take any meat into the Hindu College where we were going to be quartered. On our way to Trincomalee, we came across a herd of wild boar that crossed us on the main road at Habarana. Our vehicle accidentally hit an animal and instead of leaving it behind, we picked it up and took it to Trincomalee. One of my Warrant Officers took it to one of the hotels and got it cooked, thereby making certain that we did not take any meat, but we did take with us cooked food!

In Trincomalee, our main requirement was to be present at all times in order to quell any impending riot. Our presence was crucial: we patrolled the streets to indicate that we were present and ready to take action if required. The protesters carried out the 'anti Sri campaign' by sitting down at various places and performing *satyagrahas*.

The year 1958 was no less important. It was on 9 and 10 June 1958, that for the first time ever, the armoured vehicles of the Ceylon Army publicly fired. The venue was none other than Galle Face Green. The reason was that we had no range in Panagoda (the main army camp) to shoot powerful shots from the armoured vehicles. An unanimous decision was taken, and as a result we agreed to place a few targets in the sea and subsequently, shot a few rounds from Galle Face Green. Prior to this event, we had asked the navy to clear the fishermen in the vicinity. The word spread all around Colombo that armoured vehicles were going to fire and in the end we had a large crowd to witness the shooting.

In the late 1950's, I served as a Field Observer of the UN Observation Group in Lebanon. This was only two years subsequent to the raising of the 1st Recce Regiment. It was a time when fierce fighting that would eventually engulf the area, had first erupted in Lebanon, between the numerous forces there. Israel was also involved. We were invited by Lebanese officials to dinner during where a dish which was considered a delicacy in the country was laid on the table. I must admit that it appeared rather appetizing. It was to my horror that I soon found out later that it was raw liver! Aghast at the prospect of eating it, I was able to tuck the serving into my pocket. My friend ate it, only to throw it up much later.

In 1962, I was dispatched for a Staff Training Course at Camberly, UK. During this period, the opportunity to follow courses abroad was rare and the experience proved valuable for any career officer. I commenced the course while living in the Officers' Mess. My neighbour was a Nigerian: Major Yakubu 'Jack' Gowon. Jack was from a well-known and affluent family in Nigeria. We met very often on our way to the halls of study and this resulted in us becoming firm friends. Myrtle joined me soon afterwards and we were fortunate to rent out an excellent flat in the countryside, at five guineas a week, the best available for the price. This however meant that my daily meetings with Jack had to come to a close, but we did invite him for meals of rice and curry prepared by Myrtle, which he always relished. A short while later he went to Germany during a short vacation and returned with the latest model Mercedes car coloured green! No one except Jack owned a Mercedes at Staff College and before long he invited us to accompany him to Edinburgh for the annual Army Tattoo. We were naturally as keen as he was to witness the 'Tattoo,' but I had to explain that it was beyond what I could afford with the meagre allowance I was receiving – even a few days in Edinburgh especially during festival time were costly, and I thought it quite beyond my means. Jack however insisted that we come and we had no choice but to keep him company. We spent five days in Edinburgh and enjoyed the Army Tattoo, a splendid occasion held at the old Edinburgh castle. It was there that he and I became close friends – Jack was easy to get on with and without doubt, a dependable friend. At the end of the course Jack went back to Nigeria and we lost contact for a while. He however informed me that he was to be married, but our correspondence was rather irregular once he became President of Nigeria.

On my return, after successfully completing the course at Camberley, I was appointed the second-in-command, 1st Reconnaissance Regiment, Ceylon Armoured Corps. Subsequently, I had a term at Army Headquarters as the General Staff Officer Operations before my appointment as Commanding Officer, 1st Reconnaissance Regiment.

I was then a Lieutenant Colonel commanding the senior regiment of the army. It was at that moment in time that I was appointed by then Prime Minister Sirimavo Bandaranaike, as the Coordinating Officer of Kegalle District, during the worst period of the JVP insurgency which erupted, wreaking mayhem and disorder in the country in 1971.

Insurrection 1971

The JVP insurrection of 1971, like a hurricane unleashing death and destruction in its path, came in the wee hours of 5th April, in all but two of the nine provinces in the island.

The Districts of Kegalle and Anuradhapura experienced the worst of the insurrection which on the whole was not a complete surprise, except for its fury and the intensity of the violence. Troops and the police were neither experienced enough nor trained to handle an insurrection of this scale and intensity. However, its strength and direction dissipated just as quickly as they came. Estimates vary but a guesstimate would ascertain that over 16,000 JVP youth were arrested or had surrendered to the security forces, police or to other agencies.

The insurrection was experienced in all except the Northern and Eastern provinces. In the other seven provinces; Kegalle and Ratnapura Districts of the Sabaragamuwa Province, Anuradhapura and Polonnaruwa Districts of the North Central Province, Kurunegala District of the North Western Province, the Matale and Kandy Districts of the Central Province, the Moneragala District of the Uva Province, Galle and Hambantota Districts of the Southern Province, and Gampaha, Kalutara and Colombo Districts of the Western Province faced the major theatres of the insurrection. The seriousness of the insurrection can be judged from the mere, yet startling, fact that 93 police stations were attacked in the week between 5th and 11th April 1971.

Reports received by the government long before April 1971, mainly from police investigating sources, stated that an armed insurrection was being planned by a select group of youth. However, this report was left unheeded or was shelved. In a report submitted to the Criminal Justice Commission (Insurgency) Inquiry No 1, the IGP stated that Special Branch Criminal Investigations Department (CID) reports indicated that about two years prior to 5 April 1971, groups of young persons between the ages of 18 to 25 were meeting in secret. These groups were active in many parts of the island. They had met in secret and discussed the existing political, economic and social conditions in the country. These groups had been organized in the form of cells, each consisting 5 to 24 members, mainly unemployed educated youth from poor families. Leaders of the organization instructed them in the form of a series of lectures which analyzed the causes of frustration among the youth and advocated a remedy that necessitated the overthrow of the government using violence. The government was also informed by the CID that members of the group were trained in the jungles and remote areas, in the basics of jungle warfare such as survival techniques, living off the land with very limited resources including food, rope climbing, self defence methods etc. There were incidents reported of thefts of weapons mostly of shot guns and cartridges from estate owners and planters. They made certain that explosives such as dynamite were secured. It was unfortunate that at that stage, the government had preferred to ignore or maybe had wished the reports away. After the general election of '70, the new regime was more engaged in enjoying the fruits of victory than in the security of the country. The reports were often dismissed as speculation although the police had recovered maps, diagrams/sketches, and data relating to police stations and military establishments, arms and ammunition dumps from the JVP, and made arrests. This attitude of the Government is one reason why the insurrection, when it did come, took nearly everyone by surprise.

The JVP was an ultra Marxist party led by Rohana Wijeweera who was a dropout from Patrice Lumumba University in Moscow, Russia. The JVP was organized into Central Committees, Coordinating Committees, District Committees and Secretaries to plan, train, and lead the 'revolution' which they interpreted as a 'class struggle.' The cadres were trained in firearms, explosives and tactics. Meetings ranging from a series of five lectures educated the youth on the problems faced by the country. The five 'lessons' were popular: the first was about the 'economic crisis,' the peasant farmer and the scarcity of land; The second lesson dealt with the 'so called independence.' The third dealt with the scourge of 'Indian expansionism,' including that of Indian labour. The fourth was about the failure of the 25 years of the 'Left' movement, and lastly and most importantly, the fifth, dealt with the revolution.

There was also a wide range of JVP news sheets and publications: *Kamkarupuwath* (Workers' News), *Janatha Vimukthi*, (People's Liberation), *Ginipupura* (The Spark), *Rathubalaya* (Red Power), *Rathulanka* (Red Lanka), *Tharuna Satana* (Youth Struggle), *Virodaya* (Challenge), *Rathu Kekulu* (Red Bloom) and a Tamil paper, *Tholilali Seydi* (Workers' News) published in racy and vibrant language making certain of sparking even a remote flicker of interest in any reader. What was perhaps the most effective were their poster and the graffiti, which started appearing islandwide with radical and militant messages and slogans meant to be read by the ordinary rural people and youth. Fiery JVP speeches aimed at the grassroots village audiences, for instance the lecture series on soil erosion and wasteland, hit the very heart and aspirations of the rural people. They also spoke eloquently of Indian intervention and how Indian estate labour, often adjacent to Sinhalese villages, threatened the employment opportunities of native Sri Lankans.

The JVP was not content with mere discourse. Posters and graffiti – the 'writing on the wall' – started to appear overnight throughout the island, except in the Northern and Eastern Provinces. This aspect of overnight appearance of the same posters bearing the same style only served to point to an organization which was orchestrated and well-disciplined. After each meeting, large or small, the members of the audience were made to contribute to the cause, by JVP youth, who carried 'tills and collection boxes.' The donations were not only of a monetary nature. There were those, including female university students, who donated their gold earrings and bangles for the cause. Some of these were organized theatrics on the part of the JVP and undeniably they proved to be effective means of winning over the people. In reality, they had never hoped to collect the finances to meet the requirements for an islandwide revolution in this manner, but it certainly created an innate sense of sharing and comradeship. It also helped as a smokescreen and cover to conceal the finances obtained by theft and robbing rural banks and payrolls of school teachers, industrial establishments and plantations. This on the other hand proved to be a rather lucrative exercise as the monies obtained in this manner ran into huge amounts.

A visible escalation of violence and defiance by the youth - the likes of which had not been witnessed earlier in the island - was seen for the first time in '71. Slowly incidents started to spiral out of control. On 10 March, the media reported an explosion in Nelundeniya in the Dedigama electorate, which killed six persons who were engaged in bomb making.

Amidst all the confusion and terror that was being unleashed, a significant event was the arrest of JVP Leader Rohana Wijeweera on 12th March. He was later transferred to Colombo from the Batticaloa Prison. On 16 March he was transferred to the former Dutch Fort - Fort Hammenheil - built on an island guarding the Jaffna Fort.

Around this time army headquarters had issued a signal to all units to use 'maximum' force instead of the usual 'minimum' force, but the officers and men were still not placed on alert. By this time, the sense of urgency had increased, prompting the government to declare a state of emergency on 16th March.

But that was not the end. A few days later, an explosion ripped through a hall of residence building at the University of Peradeniya, The police recovered bombs and large quantities of explosives and weapons. Uniforms were in the process of being stitched in a women's hall of residence and similar uniforms were recovered from other areas along with shot guns and explosives. The uniforms had a familiar style with four large shirt pockets, and were blue in colour. Further investigations unearthed a transmitter.

The University of Peradeniya by the year 1970 was a well-known hotbed of JVP proliferation and this situation was not one that materialized overnight, as signs of violence were distinguishable as far back as the 1960's. The first indication was the emergence of aggression amongst the existing student Marxist elements supported by a sympathetic staff. Some of the staff too had Marxist leanings and aired their own differences of opinions with the authorities but their methods were limited merely to discussions and 'strikes;' never resorting to violence or destruction. Most, if not all, strikes were means of entertainment and occurred frequently during the first term of the academic year. Severe violence started becoming noticeable only from the latter part of the 1960's. The ragging of students became not only violent but unbearable, resulting even in students committing suicide. There seemed to be a feeling of vindictiveness due to the prevalent frustration and disparity in social standards. Violence, therefore, seemed to be the only expression of 'freedom.' The influx of 'external' students lodged unofficially in the halls of residence provided a further discontented element. In 1968, prior to the Independence Day celebrations on 4 February, the Campus was selected to provide accommodation to the army as the Armed Services Parade was to be held in Kandy. Instead of a warm welcome, the students mounted a violent attack on the troops with stones and homemade 'weapons.' One soldier was severely wounded and hospitalized with head injuries. There was little the University staff could do to calm the students.

I, myself, had made arrangements to participate in the Independence Day Parade in Kandy. My troops were in Kandy with the armoured cars. Meanwhile, I went with some Ferret scout cars to make sure that the students were sent back to the halls of residence. I still recall personally driving a car, while chasing students who were gathered in pockets throwing stones at the troops. But the presence of troops and armour had the desired effect on the students, who hastily dispersed. I had an interesting person named Sergeant Ousman amongst my troops who was not content to sit and watch the disruption – he collected a few stones and threw it back at the students. The students in turn ran away. According to information received at a much later stage, even at that stage, the JVP was trying to rehearse the build up for the '71 insurgency. This does seem rather far-fetched, I agree, but one never could say...

The JVP was undeniably well-organized and prepared. The first of the coordinated plan to attack police stations was on the Wellawaya Police Station on the night of 4th April. The date and time originally scheduled for this attack was the night of the 5th, but this was misinterpreted by the Moneragala JVP group leader on the 4th night. It is now known that the final decision was taken by the nine senior JVP members on 2nd April to attack almost all the police stations within 24 hours starting from the night of 5th April 1971. This meeting was held at the Vidyodaya University, formerly the Vidyodaya Pirivena, a seat of learning exclusively for Buddhist monks to study Pali, Sanskrit the Buddhist texts. University status had been granted to the Pirivena by the SLFP government. It was at this very location that the decision was taken to attack the very government which had accorded it this status. The decision had to be conveyed immediately to the regional leaders. That was not an era of the cellular telephone or of advanced telecom facilities. The senior leaders thus received a telegram in the coded form stating "JVP Appuhamy expired, funeral 5th", which was misunderstood by the JVP hierarchy in Wellawaya assuming that this indicated that the attack should take place on the night of the 4th. As luck would have it, this attack which, so to speak, jumped the gun, alerted the armed forces and the police giving them 24 hours lead time to prepare when the actual coordinated attack on 92 police stations in the early hours of the 5th was unleashed.

An urgent Security Council meeting was summoned which was attended by the Governor General, the Prime Minister, the service commanders and the IGP. An operations room was set up at Temple Trees the residence of the Prime Minister. This subsequently became the operations headquarters until the end of the insurrection. With the establishment of the operations room, radio messages were sent to all military and police stations that an attack was imminent on the night of the 5th, warning them to be prepared.On the 9th night, the police from Dedigama, Mawanella, Aranayake, and Rambukkana were withdrawn to defend the Kegalle Police Headquarters. Food and ammunition arrived by means of air force helicopters which landed on the police parade ground as the roads were being controlled by the JVP insurgents.

On 10th April 1971, I was ordered to report to Prime Minister Mrs. Sirimavo Bandaranaike at Temple Trees. This order took me by surprise, as I was not informed of my mission either by the Army Commander or by the Army Headquarters as was the practice, and the procedure that was being followed, by any means, was not traditional. As the Commanding Officer of the 1st Recce Regiment, I knew of the tragic events that had occurred during the first few days of the insurgency, but had no idea about the immediacy and the significant nature of the particular task which I was to be assigned to undertake.

On arrival, I was met by the Assistant Secretary, former IGP S.A. Dissanayake, and Army Commander General D.S. Attygalle in the Operations Room. The Prime Minister spoke to me in the presence of Mr. Lakshman Jayakody, her Deputy Minister Defence, and proceeded to brief me on the situation especially in the Kegalle District where all police stations except the major one in Kegalle town was overrun.

The turn of events was such that in the face of such peril, I was appointed the Military Coordinating Officer of the Kegalle District with immediate effect and ordered to Kegalle forthwith. Though I knew of the dangers to be faced, I was proud to accept this challenging task, as the 1st Recce Regiment was raised to provide mobility and this was to be the test, being the first military operation, for my unit. I had benefited from sound knowledge and training in handling these situations in the jungle training at Far Eastern Land Force (FARELF) in Malaysia. This gave me the confidence to 'get on' with the task, especially once the Prime Minister issued orders and appointed me personally as the Coordinating Officer for the Kegalle District. The challenge stared in my face; the task entrusted to me was one that had no option except to be successful in the end.

It was rather unusual that the assignment would be to the Kegalle District as my ancestral home was in Mawanella just a few miles away. Mawanella was also one of the worst affected areas of the insurgency. The danger was more imminent for me as my parents, relatives and friends also lived in Mawanella. Today, the location of my home -Erabudupela - just two miles from the main Colombo-Kandy Road, is developed and heavily populated but it was not so in 1971. It is the practice of insurgents the world over to launch reprisals on 'soft' targets as a means of coercion against law enforcement authorities. The only precaution I was able to take was to safeguard my mother who was evacuated almost immediately to live with my brother, Chandra. I remember that by 1600 hours, my troops with a convoy of World War II vintage Daimler armoured cars, Ferret scout cars and a few soft skinned vehicles (known as B vehicles in the army) left for Kegalle on the A1 Road on 10th April. This road, always very busy, was then deserted. After about the halfway mark in the little town of Warakapola the road was obstructed by trees, cut down across the road by insurgents to obstruct and delay the advancing troops. There was the added disadvantage of halting the 'soft' skinned vehicles, which would offer the insurgents an easy target. Nevertheless, road clearing had to be done, however tedious and dangerous, and with the help of our practiced drills, we soon reached our first destination, the Kegalle Police Station, around 1900 hours; a journey which under normal circumstances would have taken merely two hours. I sat on the turret of a Scout car parked opposite the District Judge's Chambers occupied by Senior Superintendent of Police (SSP) Ana Seneviratne and Government Agent (GA) K.H.J. Wijedasa. It did not take very long for Wijedasa to inform me that I was attempting suicide by sitting on the turret. The advice, I must say, was well taken!

I was briefed by K.H.J. Wijedasa, Ana Seneviratne, and the Army Detachment Commander about the state of affairs. The situation appeared worse than what I already knew and expected. There was no government administration whatever in the entire district. What belonged to the government was restricted to the three acres of land which housed the Kachcheri, the Police Station and the premises of the Courts of Law. There was 'intense activity by the insurgents at night' around this complex. The people were in a state of panic and the stocks of food and essential items such as kerosene needed replenishment. Agriculture, plantations and industries had come to a grinding halt. The insurgents had destroyed the Warakapola Police Station on the 8th and captured two submachine guns and five rifles. Bulathkohupitiya, Aranayake, Mawanella, Pindeniya, Rambukkana and Dedigama Police Stations had been attacked and abandoned. The Police Stations at Aranayake and Warakapola were completely destroyed by fire. The insurgents had established themselves well in Aranayake, Dedigama, Morontota and were dominating these areas according to their own rules. They had their own transport system and their own courts of law where civilians were indicted. These methods are adopted by all insurgent/terrorist organisations to create a sense of normalcy and confidence in the people that they and not the government are in control. The Liberation Tigers of Tamil Eelam (LTTE) has also adopted similar tactics to expose the ineffectiveness of the government machinery. The LTTE took years to establish courts of their own but the JVP did it within a few days of their initial attack. The Kegalle District was without electricity and they did not have telephone facilities when the army arrived. However, the army had its own system of communications via radio links with Colombo.

My primary task after arriving in Kegalle and after being briefed by the Government Agent and the Superintendent of Police was to gather all available information and intelligence of JVP activities in the Kegalle District. I summoned the government agencies and the Grama Sevakas and asked them to inform me of the problems they had and the issues they were facing.

There was information that the Kegalle Hospital was under threat by the insurgents and the medical staff was reluctant to work. As an essential service, it had to be provided with security. Any disruption to the hospital service would have demoralized the entire district as well the soldiers who were injured in operations. The situation was serious and it required my personal attention for the medical staff to continue work. The senior medical staff was committed to work, but the problem was at the junior levels, and at the level of hospital minor staff. Security was therefore provided by troops and the police although they were also under severe strain.

The briefings I received from K.H.J. Wijedasa and Ana Seneviratne, when I first arrived in Kegalle, was useful. Every night, as Coordinating Officer, I met the GA, SSP, staff officer/s, and government representatives who were available and planned operations. I am grateful to these others for their advice and caution. I also attended weekly meetings with the Prime Minister, the service commanders, the IGP and other officials at Temple Trees operations room. I was also fortunate to have the company of CLI troops commanded by Major Tony Rajudeen. The infantry was equipped with the 303 Light Machine Gun, 2" mortar and the 38 pistol with the old 'pack' with web belt, anklets and Khaki uniform and the ill fitting steel helmet. Movement was restricted with a heavy pack with over a 30-kilo load.

The situation report to Temple Trees and Army Headquarters on 11th April '71 at 0700 hours was: "All police stations except main station in Kegalle have been closed. No night patrolling is done." Insurgents were on rampage in certain areas both during day and night. Immediate operations were carried out to clear the vicinity. It is significant that no night patrolling was undertaken as troops are especially vulnerable to insurgents equipped with better knowledge of the terrain.

The report sent to Temple Trees and Army Headquarters at 2015 hours after the first engagement on the 12th reported heavy opposition. Though we met with heavy resistance, we were able to counter the attack. The attacks however indicated what was to be expected. It is natural for the opposing insurgents to give off the best in their arsenal to weaken the resolve of the forces, but such attacks also offer a good idea of enemy weapons, tactics, determination and morale to plan future operations. It was clear the insurgents were reasonably well trained in the use of firearms, field craft, guerrilla tactics, and had numerical superiority. Seven casualties were evacuated to Colombo. The first combat death, that of Private Ranasinghe JDW of the Ceylon Light Infantry demoralized troops for a while as until then they had never witnessed casualties.

The army began with road clearing operations prior to conducting aggressive patrolling. Major M.H. Gunaratne CAC was detailed to conduct a 'fighting' patrol consisting of a Scout car, a three tonne truck and two jeeps on the Mawanella–Aranayake Road occupied by insurgent forces. The second in command was Captain J.B. Pagoda of the CLI occupying the 3rd, vehicle with Sergeant Mahipala in the last vehicle. There was intelligence that at Ussapitiya the enemy was deployed in strength and the meandering road was ideally suitable for ambush. The patrol encountered a hail of homemade explosive devices injuring Corporal Kithsiri and Major Gunaratne, but the offensive was continued and completed by Captain Pagoda and Sergeant Mahipala. The enemy finally dispersed after about 15 minutes, leaving behind two dead. The attack was not pursued as there was no provision for casualty evacuation or for the replenishment of ammunition. Once again it was evident that the insurgents had a sound knowledge of the terrain and a shrewd sense of field craft confirming the earlier assessment that most of them had been trained. Another patrol led by Captain U.A. Karunaratne of the CLI in three jeeps with 12 men and the Executive Engineer were ambushed on their return at Walakade in Uthuvankande by about 75 terrorists with rifles, sub machine guns, shot guns and homemade bombs. One soldier died and six others were wounded. It was the first instance the terrorists laid an ambush on the Colombo-Kandy Road, blocking the road with a lorry and at a well selected site.

On the 14th a mobile patrol again led by Captain J.B. Pagoda with a platoon of about 30 men encountered stiff resistance in Aranayake town which was overcome, but the patrol was ambushed again with shot guns, rifles and handmade bombs from the Ussapitiya school premises between the two narrow bends on the road. Ahead of the school was a precipice of 50 degrees, but troops assaulted the ambush group, which was later reliably learnt to have consisted of over 100 insurgents. Unfortunately, Private Ran Banda was killed in action and Captain Pagoda suffered severe gun shot injuries. He was convinced that the insurgents had mastered the ambush technique which 'can be expected only from professionally trained soldiers.'

Operations were planned based on the briefings and intelligence reports. My system of operation has always been through intelligence. Otherwise it would be groping in the dark and suffering unexpected high casualties in the process. For intelligence, my strategy was that one must use all available resources. It could be a beggar on the street or, a lady teacher; basically it could be anybody who can give you information! Subsequently, a cell called the "int cell" was formed to collect all the information, put it together and proceed to identify the target. That, in short, was the full time job of my intelligence officer and two or three others.

I did not have an intelligence team but I quickly established one when I took over. An intelligence 'cell' with some police elements was established with an officer of the Cadet corps who was mobilized for 'active' service due to the shortage of regular officers at Coordinating Headquarters. The duty of this cell was to gather and disseminate intelligence to where it was required. I set about this by contacting all government agencies including the village headmen (now known as *Grama Sevakas*), public sector and private sector individuals. Through this process we received information about individuals in the area who were reliable and would give genuine information. Selected informants were given security passes to come to my headquarters anytime during curfew and I briefed the police and armed forces about this arrangement.

In addition to this I also encouraged all detachment commanders and others to do the same and pass on information as quickly as possible. I went through the intelligence gathered as often as possible during the day and at the end of the day an intelligence summary was prepared by the Intelligence Officer. Having discussed the intelligence with the senior officers and the police I planned the operations for next day. Whilst conducting the operation next day we gathered further information about the movements and hideouts of the insurgents. These were confirmed by the information gathered through the civil population. We then took on the target without wasting time. This is how the intelligence system worked, and no operations were planned nor undertaken without proper intelligence.

As a result of collecting information, operations brought out immediate results which were welcome by the general public. As a result we received credible information. We selected the most vital targets of the JVP that intensified the problems of the Kegalle District. I took them on with all available troops. Operations were not in the form of major attacks against JVP camps as there were no such camps except for those in Rambukkana and one or two in Dedigama and Moronthota. What we did to capture the insurgents was to lay a fair number of ambushes in vital areas and places in which we got information. For example, we would get information on how the insurgents got their food, how they moved from village to village. We laid ambushes based on such information and these were often very successful. The ambushes could not be carried out without getting the troops to be absolutely vigilant. The system of communication in the ambush party had been taught to every soldier. If the enemy is arriving and the person who sees them first will give a tug, then the message goes down to the last member of the group lying in ambush.

The ambushes were set as late as possible in the evening and the troops got into positions and stayed in the ambush without a murmur and got the targets. The insurgents thought that they had the run of the land in the night. Our ambushes were well set and organized and if the insurgents passed through they would definitely be dead. On the contrary if the target did not turn up, the ambush party would abandon the mission and leave.

With the law and order situation improving steadily and with incidents restricted to minor ones, operations were extended to the remoter areas of Morontota, Dedigama and Randeniya in the Kegalle District to root the insurgents out. The main task which remained was the removal of the huge trees that were cut down and placed across roads. The problem of approaching the target was difficult especially in the periphery because there were a large number of obstacles on the road. To get to the target we had to clear the obstacles which took a long time and made a lot of noise! In other words, it was like ringing bells to say that we were coming. This gave adequate notice to the insurgents to disappear from the area. One such incident that I recollect was on an attack in Moronthota (based on information that a fair number of insurgents were operating there). I went myself. There were a large number of obstacles we had to clear before we got there. Even on the way we noticed that people were very happy that we were coming there and they gave us information. But the most amusing thing was that I walked around a large closed down building, but never bothered to attempt to open the door. We finished the operation and came back very late in the evening, only to be told that there were more than hundred insurgents in that large building that I walked around. They didn't shoot at me nor did I try to open the door. They had escaped and disappeared completely out of the Kegalle District. It was a costly miss out, on our part.

The JVP attacks directed against the forces had failed but sporadic attacks continued. They killed anyone whom they suspected to be informants such as village headmen and government officials, but did not interfere with the families of the security forces as they were expecting the cooperation of the armed forces. Probably some army and navy personnel including officers had been JVP members, who did not identify themselves as the insurrection was a lost cause.

Army operations conducted between 13th and 20th April killed or dispersed the JVP cadres and subsequently we were able to re-establish the police stations. The re-establishment of police stations was a priority. The nine police stations which were overrun were re-established in available accommodation and work commenced to renovate those destroyed. Meanwhile, the support of the people was required and their help in rebuilding was both inspiring and encouraging. They realized that terror could be defeated only by group participation. Dedigama was one of the hotbeds of insurgency in the district and its police station was destroyed on the night of the 5th. I spoke to Mr. Dudley Senanayake, former Prime Minister, who was the Member of Parliament for the area since Independence, and he promptly agreed without even the slightest suggestion from me to repair the police station on his own account.

I deployed troops to work with the police immediately in the newly established temporary police stations. This restored public confidence in the police as well in the army – a good base to begin my work. I also set up Vigilance Committees consisting of local leaders cooperating with the village headmen. Frequent meetings with the people in Kegalle town and in the suburbs and villages were helpful to read the situation at first hand. These activities enabled us to build a reliable intelligence system for anti-insurgent operations. With success against the insurgents, there was no difficulty in getting valuable intelligence unlike in the initial stages.

We also trained a large number of home-guards through the local police as well as village headmen. These were personnel who were working in the village and they were able to give accurate information on any suspicious activities through the local police stations. They were given shot guns without which they would have found it difficult to protect themselves.

Meanwhile, I organized what in military terms are called *Low Intensity* operations against the insurgents. *High intensity* operations are conducted in a manner where the soldier hits hard at each and every target. The rebels are captured and neutralized. *Low intensity* operations however consisted of ambushes and very active fighting patrols, patrolling to keep the lines of communications clear of insurgent activities, especially to allow the essential items including food to move. These operations did not permit the insurgents any time to regroup their forces, as you take on anything that appears. We kept the insurgents on the move. We never gave them a chance to re-group. Our strategy was to keep them on the move and trap them in the ambushes.

It was at this time that we received the new Saladin armoured cars, and field firing training exercises targeting Bible Rock were conducted, witnessed by the villagers. This not only helped train the troops but had a tremendous effect in demoralizing and terrifying the insurgents. They either surrendered or retreated north. However, we did not use armoured cars for active firing. Unless you have a very good target and you are very sure of your terrain, you cannot take the chance of firing at an armoured car; it could kill some innocent people. We did fire the armoured cars in selected areas that we were absolutely sure of. I used both armoured cars and infantry mortars. Mortars are area weapons as opposed to a direct fire weapon of the armoured car. We fired a few mortar rounds into areas where the terrorists were, but we never fired unless we were 100% sure of the safety of civilian settlements and houses. When used at night, the mortar has a tremendous affect on the morale of the enemy. They do not understand which direction it came from and when it will come again. The purpose of the mortar apart from killing the insurgents is to create panic among them. I always believed that you must fire at the enemy when he least expects it!

A few vignettes do come to mind when I think about operations: The first is of which would be about the insurgent who had been ordered to kill me. After a few days of intensive operations many insurgents had been captured and kept in cells prior to sending them for further investigations. Among them was a 25-year-old who stated that he had been assigned to assassinate the Coordinating Officer. Unaware to whom he was speaking, he revealed that he had come upon a few opportunities but had not received final orders.

The captured insurgent, about whom I spoke before, confessed to having been misled into believing that the army was only meant to kill but had realized it was not so. Indoctrination is an effective weapon to mislead, which is why troops must interact with the people. It is clear that if operations are impartially conducted with equal justice, it would not take long to win public support. What will bring results is to do what is expected from the armed services, which is one's duty. This need not be deliberately targeted to 'win hearts and minds' using special 'confidence building measures' as they are known today, as 'you cannot fool all the people all the time.' The emphasis should not be only on weaponry but on good leadership.

Two other incidents stand out because they involved similar complaints but with vastly differing outcomes. First was an urgent call from the Kegalle Convent Mother Superior around midnight at the height of the insurgency. A few of us were still working and we decided to investigate with the few weapons and a light machine gun we had as the Mother Superior sounded desperate. It turned out the insurgents had walked into the pantry and stores, ransacked what they could and carried away the provisions meant for the hostellers. We mounted the machine gun on the parapet wall, fired a few rounds into the rubber plantation in the neighbourhood and vigilance was maintained throughout the night. To our surprise, in the morning when we searched the area, we found we had fired into some insurgents as we recovered a few dead armed insurgents in uniform with their weapons.

Again, a few days later a request was made once again late at night by an industrialist who was provided with two security men armed with shot guns. Once again we proceeded to his complex which was opposite the convent. He showed us a light, well below his house and tried to point towards some insurgents in the cemetery below. However, I was not convinced that the light was being used by the insurgents; but I decided to fire a shot myself in the direction to ascertain the reaction. A few minutes passed. I decided to investigate, accompanied by a few troops. I instructed my men not to fire until I ordered them to, or only if absolutely necessary to do so. To my horror the house belonged to an innocent family with a child. They were deeply shocked and I was able to calm their fears by apologizing to them profusely for my indiscretion. Shocked and indignant, I immediately sent out a party to withdraw all the weapons I had permitted the industrialist to possess.

The following morning I had many appeals including a visit from the private secretary of the then powerful Minister and the Kegalle MP, Mr. P.B.G. Kalugalle, on behalf of the industrialist. I refused those appeals but suggested to the industrialist that if he felt insecure he should move out of his house and live elsewhere with his family, which he did. This incident helped send a strong message to the public – that the security forces **will** do its duty without being influenced by politicians. There were naturally a few complaints against the security forces but these were summarily dismissed after case by case investigation. We also refused to accept any gifts, even of food or fruit, and advised the donors to meet the GA and the AGA's on how these should be distributed to the people who required them.

The civilian administrative complex consisting of the Kachcheri, Police Headquarters, SSP office, law courts, court offices, and the judges' chambers were all located in a small compound. It was worse than the Pettah market! It was terribly crowded. There were vendors around the area as well. I realized that limited space restricted official work and was not conducive to efficiency in the transaction of public business. This prompted me to select an abandoned building complex that included the former hospital in close proximity to town which was in reasonably good condition to accommodate many of those public offices. The District Judge of Kegalle, Mr. Amerasinghe was a very nice person. I discussed with him the feasibility of the courts complex moving to the former hospital. He was really taken up with the idea of moving the courts. The lawyers at first were hesitant to accept the new idea, especially when it came from a serviceman. After discussions with the District Judge and lawyers, I discussed the idea with the Prime Minister at one of our weekly meetings. She agreed to the suggestion after consulting with Justice Minister Felix Dias Bandaranaike. I employed the arrested insurgents to clean the buildings including the approach road. The shifting of the courts complex eased the working environment of the Kachcheri and the police. The lawyers also soon realized that the shift was a good idea as the litigants had sufficient space to move freely.

The security situation continued to improve. Those responsible for the distribution of food and essential items to the public were able to organize themselves better to reach the people who required these essential items. By the 29th, all JVP fighting units consisting of about 130 cadres, left their stronghold at Balapattawa and retreated from the Kegalle District.

My next meeting with the Prime Minister paved the way for further success. She showed particular interest in the welfare and progress of the 'surrendees' and considered this as her personal project and responsibility as they had answered her call to surrender. I had briefed her that a few of the insurgents had 'run away' to Anuradhapura and Kantalai. Her reply was: "Why don't you pursue them and catch them there?" This was a challenge which I could not resist. Within two weeks, the Prime Minister posted me to Anuradhapura where I established a Coordinating Headquarters in a pilgrims' rest.

The insurgents moved to Anuradhapura as they thought it was a safer place with all its jungles. Anuradhapura is the biggest district in Sri Lanka. At that time people were concentrated in the city and the rest of the area was covered with thick jungle. One could easily move from one place to another through jungle without encountering any disturbance or problem. This led the insurgents to believe that this was the safest place to seek refuge from capture.

There would have been a few methods by which they found their sustenance at that time. The easiest was to use the stolen money which they had carefully accumulated. To make matters easier, food was fairly reasonably available in those areas i.e. *kurakkan* and corn. Vegetables were also cheaply available. When Anuradhapura was getting hotter than expected, their next step was to move to Kantalai and to Wilpattu.

At Anuradhapura, GA Mr. Manamperi, a very genial man, and the SSP Mr. D.T.M. Senerath, a promising athlete in his time at the University of Ceylon Peradeniya, attended my daily briefings. The Ven. Revatha Thera, the Chief incumbent of the Atamasthanaya became a great asset to me in conducting operations as his advice was constructive and valuable, cautioning me always to act with understanding and compassion. There was unanimous cooperation from other religious dignitaries as well.

We moved out to a new unoccupied building constructed for the Nurses' Training School in the New Town of Anuradhapura, which provided ample accommodation for the coordinating staff and troops including the two single engine and single seater – G47 Bell helicopters for operations.

Anuradhapura had been the capital of Sri Lanka's 'Golden age' for over a thousand years; probably the only capital to survive for such a long period. There was much to be done to improve security in the Anurdhapura District. This could not be achieved by being confined within barricades and barbed wire, which succeeded in creating a wrong sense of security in the minds of troops. The environment in the Anuradhapura District was not the same as in Kegalle. There was thick jungle in the interior, with the population being concentrated around the administrative establishments such as the Kachcheri complex, the judicial and prisons departments, petroleum depots, Transport Board depots, railway institutions, and medical and other facilities. Each of these places had to be provided with security as they were potential insurgent targets, as at this point in time the insurgents enjoyed some freedom of movement with adequate hideouts in the jungles and mountain ranges.

My decision was to establish many army detachments in remote areas to give confidence to the people and to prevent the regrouping of large numbers of insurgents planning to attack vulnerable targets. The first of these detachments were set up at Kahatagasdigiliya, Kala Oya, Galenbidunuwewa and Ottappuwa: places that were considered insurgent bases for staging operations. The system of establishing 'intelligence cells' linked to the coordinating office and detachments which proved very successful in my counter insurgency work in Kegalle District was adopted in Anuradhapura as well. Each detachment had its own intelligence 'cell' with an officer to direct its activities, instructed by the coordinating office. Intelligence affecting the coordinating officers in the adjacent areas was channelled on a need-to-know basis, which the recipients in turn reciprocated. In this manner, we obtained 'hot' intelligence to conduct immediate offensives.

The 1 Sinha Rifle Regiment under Captain Asoka Silva undertook successful operations against the insurgents with troops and policemen drawn from adjacent detachments. 'Cordon and search' counter insurgency operations and fighting patrols with large bodies of men were the most effective means of counter insurgency at this stage. This meant that the fighting patrols went searching for insurgent groups and once found, eliminated them.

The incursions into insurgent camps and areas from the detachments of Kallaru and Nochiyagama, with attached police personnel, were very effective to break the will of the few remaining insurgent groups. Air support for these operations was restricted to huge Russian built KA26 helicopters to move reinforcements speedily. Air support was also employed to pursue fleeing insurgents but their critical task was to airlift rations into the jungle bases where troops were deployed temporarily for operations. The insurgents did not possess the firepower similar to the LTTE, especially in the form of missiles, RPGs or even heavy machine guns with which to destroy helicopters. The police handled the captured/surrendered insurgents according to the legal requirements, an experience most troops at this stage did not have.

Consequently, the insurgents retreated into a difficult area of Kantalai, a vast area of forest reserve on the Trincomalee Road. There we had to carry out some in-depth patrols and search and destroy operations. We had no idea of the exact location of the camps. We had to undertake a major operation starting from the bottom and going up. Needless to say, it took us a long time. We issued the troops a 24-hour pack each and then kept on supplying them with rations. During the day they had to survive on hard rations such as biscuits and cheese etc. In the evenings they were supplied with cooked hot meals. The hot meals were dropped by the Russian helicopters. In remote areas such as the Kantalai Forest Reserve, this was the only means of access to the troops. I also have been on these helicopters quite a few times as it gave me the opportunity to meet the troops and talk to them. Otherwise, it was very difficult to be in contact with the troops.

In one of the movements of troops, they hit a marijuana plantation. The instructions given were to destroy and burn the plantation. That evening, I had decided to go in the helicopter with the food drop. When we found the place where the plantation had been found, the sight that awaited us was unbelievable! The troops were moving around, singing and waving at the helicopter. Infuriated, I asked the pilot "What the hell is going on?" The pilot responded "Sir, I can see some smoke going up." It turned out the troops had inhaled the fumes as the plantation was being burnt and as a result become intoxicated! However, they were able to clear a patch for the helicopter to land on. The singing troops were firmly instructed to have dinner and sleep it off. The next morning, though slightly groggy, they insisted on being perfectly fine!

At Kala Oya, we conducted a large-scale operation on the borders of Wilpattu. The pilot, Flight Lieutenant C.T. Gunawardena however, could not control the helicopter and was forced to make an emergency landing on the bank of the Kala Oya. At that point, I knew the landing was a matter of life and death. Fortunately, the gods were on our side! The pilot found a patch of sand he could land on. If there were any insurgents around, they would have wiped us out without any hesitation. I promptly advised the pilot to take off without me as the helicopter would have less weight. He staunchly refused to leave me behind. On my insistence he did and passed the message on radio. Meanwhile, I did not try to get too bold or start walking either. All I did was stay calm – something which was not easy to do given the situation. However, I did not have to wait too long. The troops came in search of me within a short time.

In the end, the insurgency fizzled out with the surrender of the remaining insurgents. On 29th April 1971 the government issued an amnesty and airdropped a four page "message from the government to the young men and women who had gone astray" in Sinhalese. The message was from the Prime Minister announcing a four-day amnesty with effect from 29th April until 4:00 p.m. on 3rd May. The first response came from Moneragala when a mother surrendered two sons with all the rice she had to the Army Detachment in Liyangolla in the Moneragla District. On Poson Day, a second final amnesty was granted which was effective from 7th June to 9th June 1971. The response was better than what was expected. The estimated 'surrendees' just two years after April '71 was over 13,500, and all except 4,200 were released from custody after interrogation and rehabilitation. According to A.C. Alles in *'Insurgency – 1971'* 92.8% of those released were Sinhalese between the ages 16-32 of whom 77% were between the ages 17-26 years with an average age 20 years (Alles, 1976).

The captured and surrendered insurgents were not kept in detention camps but in rehabilitation camps supervised by the government. Akkarayankulm, Polonnaruwa Royal College, Senapura Rehabilitation Centre, Vidyodaya and Vidyalankara University campuses were also turned into rehabilitation camps under the command of experienced senior officers. The food provided was reasonable with facilities for sports, bathing, education and they were also given the option of sitting for examinations. Statistics differ as to the number who went through these camps, varying from 13,000 to 18,000.

One year after the insurrection, the Prime Minister who was also the Minister of Defence was content. While entertaining the Coordinating Officers to tea at Temple Trees, she commended the troops and the policemen who under heavy odds reacted beyond expectation to restore law and order once again. She did not miss the opportunity to remind the Army Commander that she directed all operations as the Commander had no plans of his own. It appeared to be all in fun, but one could see that she certainly meant each word that she spoke!

Much has been said and written about the army at that time. Many said that the army was only a 'peacetime' and 'ceremonial' army, which was young and inexperienced. But on looking back, we should be proud of the men who risked their lives, with little or no intelligence about the enemy, and armed with only World War II vintage weapons. The country was fortunate for the communication gap which resulted in the premature JVP attack on 4th April night on the Wellawaya Police Station, which alerted the security forces and the police and provided a critical 24-hour prior warning. But it was evident that either there was a complete intelligence failure or a total disregard by the government to warnings given by the state 'eyes and ears' intelligence agencies. During the first week, the armed forces were on the defensive, totally 'blind' with the lack of intelligence.

The numbers of injured police, army, navy and air force personnel were 194, 91, 5 and 15 respectively. The youth involved in the insurrection were largely from the majority Sinhalese community. The estimates of youth affected range from 30–60,000 killed or missing with thousands injured. Of those killed, many could be considered 'innocent' of major crimes. The damage to life, property and the misery which followed can never be estimated in rupees. The 146 JVP members who were convicted at the Criminal Justice Commission (CJC) trials were later pardoned and JVP Leader Rohana Wijeweera, who was the 13th accused, later, in an ironical turn of events, contested for Presidency.

Although reports submitted at the time declared that the JVP cadres were well-trained and attacks well-planned, it was not so with many attacks. It was not that difficult to surprise a remote police station manned by policemen who could hardly fire a .303 World War II vintage rifle. The insurgents also did not have the expertise to use explosives as was evident in the way they prepared demolitions. In many instances they tied explosives in the centre of the bridge rather than at the two ends which is the more effective way. However, hand-bomb making had become a cottage industry in the areas of Pindeniya, Dedigama and Morontota. Usually these were made from used cans of condensed milk and packed with gelignite, broken glass, nails and the barbs from barbed wire, which were freely available. The JVP were sufficiently innovative to refill their own cartridges to re-use them in shot guns with a small charge.

The insurgents' frequently used weapon was the 'Molotov Cocktail.' Many more insurgents were seriously injured using these unreliable explosives than in their direct attacks on police stations. Most of the injuries occurred when the Molotov Cocktails exploded in their faces when trying to light the guns using ordinary safety matches. Officers and senior NCOs who served at the time agree that the JVP suffered heavy casualties by trying to activate their own explosive devices. A simple case of over confidence and the lack of proper medical support cost them lives. Some of the JVP leaders who survive still carry scars of yesterday.

Two vital factors in favour of the JVP cadres were their high morale and confidence in the cause they fought for. Although poorly armed with only shot guns, homemade guns and grenades, JVP cadres were also armed with pride, motivation and dedication to a cause in which they fanatically believed. They were prepared to lay down their lives not in suicide squads and suicide missions but in frontal attacks with their largely homemade weapons and explosive devices. However ill equipped, the insurgents were also armed with an intimate knowledge of the terrain, an advantage which could have helped them overcome larger and better equipped forces, if employed effectively when maintaining their ambushes. There were also women who participated in these attacks and it is incorrect to maintain that LTTE women 'soldiers' were the first to be engaged in combat against the security forces.

In retrospect, I believe that had these JVP insurgents access to machine guns, RPGs, and other modern weaponry, the armed forces may have been hard pressed to defeat them. Ultimately, superiority in weaponry and the discipline of troops in the field was no match for the insurgents and it was a matter of time before they surrendered. More importantly, the JVP was inexperienced, without communications and a trained leadership to defeat an army endowed with the resources of a state. The JVP also did not have a firm headquarters from which to conduct operations and issue communications, and once the insurgency was launched, their leaders had little or no control of its 'foot soldiers' to direct and deploy them.

The Anuradhapura Base Camp

In discussions with Mr. Maithripala Senanayake, the Minister of Irrigation, Power and Highways and Mr. K.B. Ratnayake, Minister of Sports and Rehabilitation, both of them MPs of the area and senior government ministers as well, I advocated the building of an army camp in Anuradhapura. In my campaign against the insurgents, I had found that regardless of politics, these ministers were committed to restore law and order and allowed us to do so without any interference.

It was my opinion that an army camp in Anuradhapura was a necessity as it was a hub of insurgents and was located strategically. Such a camp would create a much needed military presence in the area. I advised the ministers to get approval from the Ministry of Defence and the Army Commander. They spoke to the Prime Minster and immediate approval was granted. We selected a location in Anuradhapura, about a mile away from the new town on the Kalaththawa Road. I spent the rest of my period in Anuradhapura constructing the army base camp with the Field Engineers and the 4th Development and Construction Engineers (4D&C) commanded by Colonel 'Pinky' Dias, a qualified engineer himself. This latter unit was known in army circles as *4 Destruction and Construction Regiment*. The construction work was in the capable hands of a committed Chartered Engineer Captain Tarsisius.

The project at first did not have budget allocations for construction work to be undertaken. This made it necessary to work closely with government agencies such as the Treasury, the Kachcheri, Forest Department, Public Works Department (PWD) and the private sector. A detailed plan was worked out by the engineer officers to accommodate a battalion group including the support arms and services. This required Officers and Warrant Officers (WO) and sergeants' messes, cooking facilities, accommodation, training areas, administrative space, transport facilities, Petrol and Oil Lubricants

(POL) dumps, water supply, vehicle repair facilities, sports areas for the troops and space for all the other needs of an army base. The manpower required for building a complex of this magnitude was immense and demanding and the labour costs would have been prohibitive. However, the discussions I had had with Minister K.B. Ratnayake as mentioned before and the Superintendent of Prisons were successful. The idea was to permit the use of JVP insurgents in custody, who were accommodated in the overcrowded Anuradhapura Prison, for the construction work. Many of them were good carpenters and masons who were willing to work while the rest volunteered as labourers. The army provided them with transport and food and after work, they were moved in vehicles for baths at the many 'reservoirs' built by the kings of the Anuradhapura period.

The cost of construction was drastically reduced as labour was now available almost free and the money thus saved was put to good use. What was remarkable about the whole project was the fact that a total of 275 young men who had been insurgents, voluntarily served with the soldiers who had hunted them in the jungles. They now worked together with a sense of comradeship. At the end of the exercise there was a bond of friendship and 'esprit de corps' and some of the former insurgents even went on to enlist as soldiers!

Senior medical officers such as Dr. Michael Abeyratne and his wife, a paediatrician, late Dr. Kamalika Abeyratne, medical officers of the Anuradhapura Base Hospital, and Major Dr. Rohan Gooneratne of the Volunteer Medical Corps actively participated in the rehabilitation work and were major players in our team. Minister K.B. Ratnayake attended many of our meetings at the Coordinating Headquarters and extended his fullest support.

The camp has proved to be a very important base camp providing security for the airfield, aircraft, troops and equipment for anti-LTTE operations today. It is also the focal point for the roads leading to Puttalam on the west and to the north and eastern coast. The complex is now beyond recognition with huge facilities serving as a training centre and barracks. The base is now also the transit point for soldiers returning from and moving to camps in the northern operational areas. The airport was also included for development as a base for air support for military operations, and now provides support for operations conducted in the Mannar, Mullaitivu, Anuradhapura and Vavuniya Districts.

Four miles away from the camp was the then abandoned Kalaththawa Farm. This farm had first acquired notoriety as the place where Alfred Soysa, of the famed Kalaththawa murders had carried out his criminal activities. It was also the venue of two important JVP conferences attended by Leader Rohana Wijeweera with three other organizers at the end of 1967. The Farm was then a large complex of abandoned land and disused accommodation then belonging to the Department of Agriculture. The GA of Anuradhapura, Mr Manamperi and some others knew that I harboured a secret passion for agriculture! So they arranged for me to take over 150 acres of land from the Kalaththawa Farm for agriculture, and the Department of Agriculture willingly released this land to me. Though it was released to me, I could not accept the land unless I retired from the army.

At the Kalaththawa Farm, my Regiment, the Armoured Corps, and its volunteer counterpart, developed and cultivated the land as many soldiers were from rural areas, and had a sound knowledge of practical agriculture and enjoyed farming. It was the time when the 'wonder' Soya and the 'winged bean' were introduced to Sri Lanka as a protein substitute for the people, especially to undernourished children. This was eagerly supported and advised on by the experts of the Maha Iluppallama Agriculture Research station established during the World War II years. This research station is known worldwide especially for its pioneering work to introduce new high yielding strains of paddy, and researchers who worked there have secured important positions in the United Nations and the Food and Agricultural Organization (FAO). The Maha Iluppallama experts got highly interested in me and the work that was being done in Kalaththawa. They came there and wanted us to grow soya beans as a model project and promised to buy every single seed that we produced at a premium price. Our labour was justly rewarded. It was indeed beautiful to see it grow.

I was able to settle a few landless ex-servicemen and their families at the farm as it developed. With time more and more families of ex-servicemen and villagers took the opportunity to settle down in the neighbourhood not only because they were landless but also they made a good security investment for the future by living around the army camp.

I was also able to plant nearly 200 high quality mango trees in the farm with the help of the agricultural extension officers. Several years later, on my way to Jaffna by road I was able to see those mango trees laden with fruit. There were of course a few senior officers who cut them to prevent any infiltration from the Tamil separatist terrorists. This action was taken not much out of necessity but due to misjudging the threat. This however was for the future. Meanwhile, mid-1971 until the end of 1972, was one of the most satisfying periods of my life as I was able to contribute something worthwhile to my country in terms of development and agriculture.

It was at the same time that I was required to meet the Prime Minister in her office at the Ministry of Defence. She discussed with me, in the presence of Deputy Minister of Defence, Mr. Lakshman Jayakody many subjects ranging from operations to what action was needed to prevent insurgency, not forgetting to inquire about my family during the difficult times of insurgency. She praised my work in Kegalle and Anuradhapaura and stated that she will nominate me to attend Royal College of Defence Studies (RCDS) and made me understand I had a bright future. During the latter part of 1972, I was informed that I was selected to attend a course at the prestigious RCDS, Belgrave Square, UK, something I had not anticipated. There was no doubt in my mind that this was her way of thanking me for my work during the '71 insurgency. This greatly encouraged me. Mrs. Bandaranaike said that many of her ministers had mentioned that my lawyer brother Chandra had joined a protest march against her government alongside then Leader of the Opposition Mr. J.R. Jayewardene. My reply was prompt - I replied that whilst it was correct that I was very close to my brother, at no time did he advice me on politics nor did I offer him legal advice. Mr. Jayakody and the Prime Minister agreed with me but advised that in my own interest my brother should be more cautious in his activities.

I was always fortunate to have absolute support in all operations during the period from my own Regiment which was handed over to my second–in–command Major M.D. Fernando with my impending departure. He needed no instructions and easily took over from me.

Royal College of Defence Studies

My course at RCDS commenced in 1973 – and what a glorious year it was - I was fortunate to be able to have my wife with me from the very start in England, but I certainly missed my two sons Niran and Rajind who were left behind.

The course is the penultimate in military studies. Participants undergoing the course are selected from the three armed services, the police and the diplomatic corps. They are posted to very senior appointments in the three services on successful completion of the one-year course. This institution is situated in Belgrave Square in London and has all the facilities, including a well-equipped library. The Commandant of this institution is a specially selected ex-service commander. In 1973, it was Air Chief Marshall Sir John Barraclough. The course content consisted mainly of strategic studies, international affairs, world economy, future trends and developments. The daily lecture was by a senior and a well-respected person of international repute who was flown in for the day's lecture and lengthy discussion that follows. We ended up with lunch with the guest speaker and spent the afternoon in the library. Royalty visits the institution once a year. Queen Elizabeth II visited RCDS in the summer and spoke to my wife and me, expressing her views on a visit to Sri Lanka, which she had greatly enjoyed.

A part of the course was a six-week tour and I selected Africa for my country visit though the USA and Asia were other options. Our African tour team consisted of about 15-16 students. These groups are led by a senior retired service officer in the RCDS staff and our group leader was a retired British Admiral. We visited the Republic of Congo, Zambia, Nigeria, Kenya and Ghana. These tours were organized so that in every country we visited we were met by government officials. The visits included the Defence Institutions of the country and briefings on their defence programs by the Service Commanders and senior staff. There was also on-the-job training. Each country entertained us with the best of traditional music and dance with drums playing throbbing music and dancers in colourful costumes.

We visited a tea estate in Kenya which, although I was quite familiar with tea, was a tremendous experience because the Kenyan plantations were different in organization than Sri Lanka's. Kenya is much larger than our own country but the British planter had a very different system most suitable and practical for the people. The Kenyans did have huge tea estates of more than 1,000-2,000 acres, but that was the exception, as much of the tea was grown by villagers in modest plots of about 2 acres within a total holding of 5-6 acres. The rest of the holding had about an acre of grass and about an acre under vegetables. The farmer usually had a dairy and the grass provided the fodder. Milk was collected in a vehicle which came on its daily rounds, and after having been tested, the representative collected it. Another vehicle did the rounds to weigh the day's pick of tea and collect and take the tea leaves to the factory for processing. A 'chit' was handed over to the owner with the weight of the tea picked for the day and another chit for the quantity and quality of the milk. These 'chits' were produced fortnightly to the centre to collect the money for the tea leaves and the milk. This system eliminated 'strikes' and the work stoppages so common here as the tea was picked by the owner and his family. Since the family members provided the labour required, the estate owners were not saddled with high wage bills. Community schools were available for the education of the children in the estates. There was another surprise for me; the machinery had the letters CCC stamped on them indicating they were made by the Colombo Commercial Company, a British company in Colombo. This also showed how the British distributed their industrial products within the empire without the need for duplication. The British planter at the site who introduced us to their tea industry had learned his trade in Sri Lanka and had served as a planter in the Sabaragamuwa Province and Bandarawela, Nuwara Eliya and Haputale.

Another memorable and unforgettable occasion was the visit to the local head of a tribe. He laid out a lavish and sumptuous banquet including delicacies made from manioc. This was prepared in the form of an *aggala* which is a familiar delicacy here in Sri Lanka, but the difference is that in Sri Lanka it is made from rice flour. We were told to have a 'go' at the food which we did without asking any questions! The entire area was dotted with beautiful homes as is familiar in the plantation districts of Nuwara Eliya, Haputale, Agrapatana, Dimbulla, and Badulla.

We travelled mostly by aircraft as long distances were involved in the tour. One day we were at the airport to begin our tour when we were cautioned to keep away from the arrival lounge as Nigerian authorities were awaiting the arrival of their President returning after a tour to China. We quickly lined up by the road but there was no large gathering as we often see in our country. The VIP motorcade was driving out, led by motorcycle outriders in ceremonial uniform when suddenly the VIP vehicle pulled up opposite me and out jumped the President, hugging and greeting me with the words: "Hello Cyril!" There was some confusion and more than a surprise for me: it was none other than my old friend General 'Jack' Gowon, President of Nigeria. The Admiral who was our tour guide announced soon after the incident, "Cyril, you are now the guide during our stay in Nigeria as you can ask anything in the world from General Jack Gowon!" General Gowon did not know that I was in the RCDS team and neither did I quite remember Jack was President of Nigeria at the time. We were hosted for tea in spite of his busy schedule. I also met General Eliya Bisala, also from Nigeria, at RCDS. He was appointed the Commandant of the Nigerian Defence Academy on his return from England at the time I was Commandant of the Army Training Centre, Diyatalawa. Shortly afterwards, Eliya Bisala wrote that he was scheduled to visit Sri Lanka with his wife. I sent him a letter and an invitation to visit Diyatalawa. However, unfortunately about two weeks later I saw an article in 'Time' or 'Newsweek' magazine, with a photograph of General Bisala wearing a white Nigerian dress being led to the seashore to be shot as ordered by their then President Obasanjo, for alleged conspiracy to depose him. Another colleague and a friend of mine at RCDS was Colonel John Stewart who later was the British High Commissioner in Colombo. He had by then retired from the British Army and had entered the diplomatic corps after successfully completing the required academic qualifications.

Diyatalawa

In August 1973, I was appointed Commander, Northern Command, based in Anuradhapura. The army at the time was deployed on the basis of Commands – Central, Western, Northern, and South Eastern, for better command and control. I took over duties at South Eastern Command (SEAC) based in Diyatalawa on 1st February 1975 and on 1st March 1976 I was also appointed Commandant of the Army Training Centre (ATC) Diyatalawa, the premier training centre of the army at the time. The 'old' Army Recruit Training Depot (ARTD) which was later the ATC had not changed much since the days I was a platoon commander. But as the Commandant of the premier army training establishment, I was responsible for the training of not only new recruits but also for all training and re-training courses for the Non Commissioned Officers (NCOs) and Young Officers, both of which categories had grown in numbers. Whereas earlier there were only 100-150 recruits training at a time, this had increased to between 300-500 and the young officers/Officer Cadets from about 10-25 to nearly 50. Today the establishment provides training facilities for about 200 Cadets.

For the NCOs one of the most important courses was the training programme known as the POT course – Potential Officer Training for NCOs, particularly for those in the rank of Lance Corporal and Corporal, which category formed the backbone of the army. The NCO is the spinal chord of the regiment providing leadership at the lowest level of command. They execute the orders, maintain discipline and provide the basis for platoons, companies, regiments, brigades, divisions and finally the army. Their training included Physical Training and there were Drill Instructor courses for Non Commissioned Officers and Warrant Officers. Warrant officers are the drill kings. All Warrant Officers are not necessarily drill instructors. But they are the ones who take the parade (i.e., leads with the sword in hand) of the squadron or the regiment. In the regiment it would be the regiment warrant officer and in the squadron it would be the squadron warrant officer. The courses are conducted in English in a very British atmosphere. Our instructors competing with the best elsewhere have performed extremely well.

The day began at the ATC rather early – often at 0600 hours or earlier. This routine was also quite familiar as Physical Training (PT) was the first on the training schedule for the day. This was so in the best military training establishments. However, today there are many who argue that PT at 0600 hours is not recommended for physical fitness especially at Diyatalawa due to the cold weather. I hold the contrary view that PT has done much good for many, judging from the experience of the hundreds if not thousands of officers and soldiers who have undergone this training. There may just a minimal few who complained or have had ill effects of such training. It certainly drilled the minds of most trainees into good habits, most of all punctuality, in beginning the day on time.

There were also firing ranges providing facilities for distances of over 1,000 yards, mortar ranges, grenade bays and the jungles within easy reach. Tactical jungle exercises lasting one month for Officer Cadets were conducted by officers and NCOs drawn not only from the ATC but also from other units such as Engineers, Artillery, Signals, Armour, Infantry and service units in the Wellawaya – Siyambalanduwa – Moneragala – Heda Oya areas. Officers and recruits lived in the jungle, organised and supervised by an enthusiastic and committed staff.

Diyatalawa was a garrison town in every sense of the word. It has a long history as this site was chosen by the British in the second half of the 19th Century to isolate the Boer prisoners of war. The 'Fox' built with white stones by the Boer prisoners, dated 1913, recall memories of the ship 'The Fox' which brought them to this island. Any visitor will not miss climbing this popularly known Fox Hill. The site was ideal as it represented the British Downs with facilities for training and recuperation. A small railway station was built for troops to embark and disembark to and from Colombo. A water tank was built prior to the war to provide for the requirements of the entire garrison town. Electricity was provided by diesel generators (spare parts were available to meet any exigencies adequate for fifty years). The British had planned for any eventuality especially the delays in shipping due to German submarine activity. The camps had accommodated thousands from the Royal Navy, and soldiers and casualties from the British Empire in South East Asia and Burma. All facilities were provided – a cinema, football, cricket and rugby grounds and even squash courts with wooden floors. They have lasted to this day. The cinema hall was reserved for soldiers, officers, their families and civilians who could find entertainment in the form of Sinhalese, Tamil and English films at a nominal rate. A well-equipped gymnasium was also established in the cinema hall with an indoor badminton court. The world's cheapest golf course provided golfers with equipment and caddies at the most reasonable rates anywhere. The Rendezvous (RV), Ella, Polo grounds and the British Services Club overlooking the RV grounds, available for troops to play with the local teams, were very popular.

Musical shows were also held on the Rendezvous grounds. There was one performance with the widest possible publicity with popular vocalists scheduled to perform, which almost ended in a fiasco as only at the last moment did the organizers realize they had not catered for the 'sound'! Last minute arrangements were made to get the equipment from Badulla about 15 miles away. The show went on to entertain the huge crowd.

The camps with corrugated roofing still survive as good as new after over a century. It would not also have been 'Diyatalawa' without the 'Army and Navy Stores' which catered for the British officers and families, 'Sethsiri Stores,' Abram Stores, Royal Saloon, Regal Cinema, the railway station and the very British looking Post Office and cottages in the heart of town. The home station of the 1st Battalion, the Gemunu Watch, the Air Force training establishment and the Survey Department officials also lived around the ATC.

The 1970's was a period of import restrictions including those on food. A dairy was established consisting of about 20 cows which provided fresh wholesome milk to all families in the garrison at very reasonable rates. There was one civilian employee who gave the best milk to the senior officers whilst diluting it for the others to earn a 'quick buck.' There was also encouragement for growing potatoes and of course tree planting including fruit trees. It was at this time that the hill overlooking the parade square was planted with cypress trees. These are now huge trees providing the background for the parades. It was a period of immense activity.

Most people in Diyatalawa were in some way linked to the services. Some were those whose sons had also enlisted in the forces and many who retired from the forces also made Diyatalawa their home as land was available. Living with the family in a very comfortable house provided by the army was enjoyable and the children loved the open spaces. Some of these children have enlisted in the services and now hold senior ranks. Many soldiers and officers who then lived in Diyatalawa, especially those who were children at the time, remember those enjoyable and rather leisurely days.

I was appointed Military Secretary on 1st January 1977. On 1st January 1978 I took over Western Command based in Panagoda and on 4th February was confirmed in the rank of Brigadier. On 1st January 1980 I was appointed Commander, Support Forces in addition to my duties as Commander, Western Command. Subsequently, on 15th February 1982 I was appointed Chief of Staff and Commander Security Forces Jaffna (SF-HQ) based at Gurunagar from September 1981 until January 1983.

Gurunagar

In the 1970s, the army had been carrying out military operations in the north to prevent smuggling and illicit immigration. Those were the two main activities the army was involved in the early years.

Activities such as smuggling, illicit immigration or the movements of terrorists across the Palk Straits were easy due to the distance between the Tamil Nadu coast and the northern tip of the Jaffna Peninsula being only one-hour by speed boat. This is also the same from Talaimmannar to the South Indian coast. Some Jaffna Tamils in this period of peace found no difficulty in racing across the Palk Strait to the southern coast for a late night movie. Coast dwelling Tamils did not consider the sea as their enemy but their friend. In those days little children were seen loitering on the seashore the entire day dipping in and out of the sea. Unlike most Sinhalese children living by the sea, the Tamil children, however small, are familiar with the tides and are able to manoeuvre a raft made of blocks of timber called '*Theppam,*' which is at times fitted with a six horsepower outboard motor. They become experts and are not afraid to dare swimming and accompanying their fathers to sea.

The 'contraband' involved in smuggling consisted of items such as spices and coconut oil in exchange for textiles and other products of Indian origin such as Nescafe etc. Electronic items became popular on the outward route, especially after the 'open economy' and liberalization of trade established since 1977.

Illicit immigration was a major problem at that time and the Task Force Illicit Immigration (TAFII) was established to control this situation. Most of the illicit immigrants were those repatriated to India under the **Sirima-Shastri Pact** (Indo-Ceylon Agreement) of 1964, and I have met some of them myself. We have caught them in the jungles and the beaches. The smugglers dropped them about 50 metres away in the sea and they had to wade through the tides. In one instance, off Mannar, in the early hours of the morning I was on the beach with my men, and we caught a few people coming in. I gave my packet of breakfast to a woman and her child. They had been at sea for 36 hours. The army presence in the north increased due to these operations. The army was guarding the coast by means of Coast Watching Posts (CWP).

There was one main army camp at Palaly. There was another camp at Kankesanthurai (KKS). The reason for this camp to be established at KKS was that it was along the main supply route by sea. KKS was used for navy patrolling and as a naval base. There was a base camp at Thalladi at the entrance to the causeway into Mannar Island and in the island itself there was the base camp at Thoddaveli.

The CWPs were right along the coasts of Mannar and the Jaffna Peninsula, linked to the main army camps. They were linked by radio and land lines laid and maintained by the army. The government made a serious mistake during the 1971 JVP insurgency, by withdrawing regular troops from the Coast Watching Points (CWP) and the Search Light Points. It was a mistake because from the late 1970s the items smuggled changed to a gun running movement of the Tamil armed youth, injured Tamil combatants, arms, explosives, ammunition, detonators and drug trafficking etc. The traditional trade and movement in illicit immigration and sarees disappeared. The smuggling was merely a prelude to people getting used to going to Tamil Nadu subsequently for military training.

This development of the armed youth and gun running across the Palk Strait has to be seen in the context of a process of radicalization of the Tamil youth developing through the 1960s and getting worse in the 1970s. In the 1960s, there would be constant black flags hoisting, *satyagrahas* and hartals. This was the environment that the Tamil youth were growing up in.

The first serious warning came in 1970 from the Superintendent of Police Jaffna Range (and later Deputy Inspector General of Police) R. Suntheralingam. He addressed a letter dated 16th November 1970 to the Inspector General of Police stating; "There is a political aspect which has also become a contributory factor for the illicit trade between Ceylon and South India, which cannot be overlooked. With the advent of the Dravida Munnethra Kazagham (DMK) regime in 1967 in India there continues a free flow of magazines propagating Tamil Nadu political ideals into Northern Ceylon via VVT (Velvettiturai). Communal extremists are capitalizing on illegal import of literature for their political activities."

Mr. Suntheralingam was born in one of the islands off Jaffna. He was a science graduate and was later attached to Interpol, at its headquarters in Paris. He was an honest, fair and impartial officer. Unfortunately his advice and warning went unheeded. The report was duly filed and forgotten. No investigations or follow up action was taken. Politicians took a long time to understand a developing situation.

In the first half of 1970, Prime Minister Sirimavo Bandaranaike, confident after her sweeping election victory in 1970, visited Jaffna. The meeting was presided by Mayor of Jaffna Alfred Duraiappah, who was a supporter of the Prime Minister. Large crowds attended the meeting as she was considered a friend, especially by the Jaffna farmers. She promoted the growing of onions and chillies, which fetched exorbitant prices as there were import restrictions on these items. The Mayor took advantage of the visit, pleading on behalf of the 42 Tamil youth arrested for violence, bank robberies and murders. He requested they be released. The Prime Minister agreed to an inquiry. When she returned to Colombo she called for the files from Mr. Ian Wickremanayake, her Legal Advisor. Superintendent of Police (SP) in charge, Mr. T.M.B. Mahat was asked for a report, but it soon came to be that it was just a formality and the Tamil youth were all released. Amongst the released were hardcore LTTE cadres.

In a strange turn of events, it was the LTTE Leader who finally killed Mayor Alfred Duraiyyapah, when he was returning from the Kovil after prayers in 1975. This was significant in 2 ways. Duraiyappah belonged to the prominent *vellala* (merchant) caste. All the political leaders of the Tamils as well as those in prominent positions politically as well as in administration were from this caste. Prabhakaran from the fisherman caste killing a *vellala* was an act of defiance against the rigid caste system. Secondly it was a sign that the youth were fed up with non-violent methods used by the Tamil leaders. Thirdly he signalled that the Tamil youth were impatient and were fed up with the elderly Tamil leadership. The LTTE Leader personally admitted he was responsible for shooting the Mayor and ironically was hailed by even the Tamil United Liberation Front (TULF) leaders, most of whom were also subsequently assassinated by the LTTE.

The Tamil youth were being regrouped into various factions and we realized that they were travelling to India for a purpose. Unfortunately, we in Sri Lanka did not have an external intelligence agency. We were operating in the blind. There was no one to brief us on both foreign and local intelligence.

Today it is a well-known fact that India began training militant groups in India in 1982–83. However, the formation and operation of radical Tamil groups started much earlier. One such example would be the attempted assassination of Minster of Post and Telecommunications Mr. C. Kumarasuriar on 10th January 1973. Another well-known incident occurred on 31st March 1973 – the interception by navy of 20,000 detonators consigned to Kuttimani, a well-known smuggler. There were a number of bank robberies, attacks on some business places and harassing of their opponents. These strings of incidents made it apparent that it was in the early 1970s that trouble started to brew.

Subsequently, after the change of government in 1977, there were reports from the Criminal Investigations Department and the Intelligence Services Department (ISD) warning the government of a military build up by the Tamil youth in the Jaffna Peninsula, encouraged and led by none other than the leader of the Tamil United Liberation Front (TULF) and Leader of the Opposition, Mr. Amirthalingam and TULF MP Mr. Yogaratnam. They publicly denounced and warned Tamil Police officers who inquired into the crimes committed by the Tamil youth informing the public openly they will "not die of natural causes." I inquired from Mr. Amithalingam many years ago about the youth going to India in boats. His response was, "Brigadier these young fellows go across and come back!" He was fully aware of what was going on. But I still maintain that he was always very friendly. He invited me many times to his house, and he was always nice and polite.

The TULF MPs were operating as usual in Parliament. They would condemn the acts of the militants to President and advice him not to take them too seriously. But at the same time they were giving patronage to the boys. The TULF MPs used to tell me, "Don't worry Brigadier. They are young boys..." Everyone was aware of the close links between the TULF leaders and the LTTE terrorist groups. The Tamil politicians gave 'safe haven' to the criminal Tamil youth in their own homes using parliamentary privilege, and by their total silence endorsed the terrorist actions.

The incidents involving Tamil militants were thus far considered merely civil disorder, and civil disorder was handled by the police. If they required our (i.e., the army's) help, then we obliged. At this stage the formation of people into different groups was at the embryonic stage. Even at this stage the Tamil 'terrorist' groups were not well-armed, nor did they have the numbers to commit themselves to any military confrontation. The different groups had to find their own income; therefore, they resorted to robbing banks. They were also killing opponents – mainly Tamils, retired policemen conducting investigations against them and attacking police stations. The core group of militants was even at that time less than 40 youth.

In 1979 Brigadier 'Bull' Weeratunga was appointed to wipe out terrorism in Jaffna. But 'Bull' himself was a problem. Though he was a close friend of mine, I am afraid to say that he did not understand the problem as I understood it. One cannot tackle an insurgency by killing and being tough on the people. That is simply the wrong way to go about it. The retaliation then would be even worse. The heavy-handedness of the government drove many Tamil youth into the hands of the terrorist groups. This resulted in the drying of support for the security forces.

During operations in the Jaffna Peninsula the intellectuals, academics and professionals were sympathetic to the activities of the armed groups whom they affectionately called 'our boys.' Lawyers appeared free in courts to defend them. The political leaders accepted them as heroes and so did the community. Religious leaders including the Bishops of Jaffna, Batticaloa, Mannar and Trincomalee and the Roman Catholic Church in general took up the cause of 'our boys.' I remember when Roman Catholic priests Fr. Singarayar and Sinnarasa and two university lecturers, Mr. and Mrs. Nithyanandan, were arrested for aiding and abetting bank robbers, these intellectuals, professionals and academics and the Roman Catholic clergy demonstrated and organized a hartal – peaceful demonstration - on a Sunday alleging torture by the security forces. One demonstrator was a leading academic who was later killed by the LTTE.

When the Roman Catholic clergy, whom the officers knew well, were asked why they organized and participated in the hartal the answer was that they had to live with their community and they were 'our' people. The chief investigator was a Roman Catholic himself now an active evangelist. These arrests were certainly to be very controversial as it gave yet another opportunity for the Eelamist separatist lobby to claim religious discrimination.

Incidentally, Mrs. Nirmala Nithyanandan was the sister of Rajini Thiranagama, who was Professor of Anatomy in the Jaffna campus, a pro- LTTE activist and sympathizer who later became disillusioned by the violence and assassinations carried out by the LTTE. She authored the book *The Broken Palmyra* which was about the realities in the Jaffna peninsula and the direction of the campaign which they once supported to redress their grievances. Her activities did not please the LTTE. She paid the penalty with her life.

The two priests, Fr. Singarayar and Sinnarasa were taken into custody for accepting the proceeds from the Neerveli bank robbery into their safe keeping. The Neerveli robbery was important in the history of Tamil terrorism. The robbery was carried out by the first armed Tamil group, known as the Tamil Eelam Liberation Organization (TELO) led by Sri Sabaratnam also known as 'Tall Sri.' After the attack which resulted in two constables being killed, the money bags were taken by two groups to their hideouts. The theoretician of TELO, Thangathurai was a youth from Point Pedro educated at Methodist College, Point Pedro, a well established American Missionary School and had passed the senior school certificate. He was a little older than the rest. He admitted he was from a family of smugglers but had not participated in the killing. He said it was Kuttimani, the 'hit man' of the group who was responsible for many ruthless killings. Ironically the Tamil United Liberation Front (TULF) nominated Kuttimani, who was a prisoner at the time, as their Member of Parliament on the death of one of their members proving overtly that the Tamil leadership was sympathetic to the cause of the violent youth. The offence was the smuggling of over 20,000 detonators from Tamil Nadu. Both Kuttimani and Thangathurai were killed in the Welikade Prison during the anti-Tamil riots in 1983.

At the time Thangathurai was in our custody a few officers were able to engage in a meaningful dialogue with him. He was a man of friendly disposition. He was from a well-to-do family in the area. Being a Marxist, more by conviction than practice, he did not believe that terrorism or assassinations could be justified in their effort to bring about an understanding with the government to redress their grievances. His grievances were also mostly in the realm of unemployment and equal opportunities in education. It was during these discussions that we found out how the LTTE was formed – the initial discussions had commenced at a reading room at VVT with Thangathurai leading the discussions along with Kuttimani and Jeggan. Politician Sivasithambaram was also said to have been actively involved.

It was also during one of these conversations he engaged in discussing the problem of the breakaway group led by the present LTTE Leader who was then just over 20 years old. Thangathurai agreed with our intelligence office that the LTTE did not have an 'educated' leadership under Prabhakaran who believed that eliminating opponents was the answer to their problems. Thangathurai suggested an alternative. He said he was innocent of any crime and opposed assassinations, and if released he will eliminate the LTTE leadership as 'Thambi' is ruthless and will drag the country into chaos.

For the record, I would like to reinstate that Thangadurai was the leader of the most senior group which is called TELO. And at that time, he was the leader and he had never touched a weapon. He was the brains behind the movement. He had entered university but hadn't qualified. What marked him was the fact that he was more a human being than a terrorist leader. He gave us information about his own group people and the leaders. Following his information, we arrested so many cadres.

By 1981, when most of the wanted people were arrested and brought in, he had given us so much of success. I recall Lionel Balagalle telling him that it was because of the information that he gave us, we arrested so many people. In return, he was asked whether there was anything we could do for him. He pondered for a while and said that his wife was in Chennai and that she was pregnant. He wanted to find out whether the baby had been born and subsequently asked to send a letter. We sent the letter and even gave a return address. I told him that in case the baby was born, to ask for a photograph. We checked the letter, which he wrote, mainly to ensure whether it was damaging to our security. We sent the letter and got a reply in 10 days. Before opening we checked there and found a picture and a letter. We checked the letter and were told that there was nothing which could harm the national security interests. We gave him the letter and for half an hour he could not speak. It was so moving for him. It was a son. At that point he was asked whether there was anything that we can do to stop this mess, since he had helped us so much until this point.

He replied saying that there was one thing to do – "keep all the people who have been arrested. But release me. I will see to it that all the other weapons are returned and that the matter ends."

This message was conveyed to the proper authorities – that was the first time a leader had been arrested and I was unable to make such a decision on my own. It had to go to the government and to the President and they did not want to take that action. They thought of the repercussions and they did not give a direct answer. I wonder if our history could have been different if Thangathurai had been released.

By that time, the military had slowly started to get involved in the activities. Until my period in Gurunagar, we found it difficult to carry on without good intelligence. The real intelligence gathering started when I was in command of Gurunagar. At the helm of this were two rather young individuals – Major Lionel Balagalle and Captain Sunil Tennekoon, who were chiefly responsible for starting the intelligence unit at Gurunagar. At this stage I was able to gain firsthand knowledge of the interior areas of the mainland. I learnt Tamil from the farmer who lived opposite the camp. The Tamil people appreciated it when they were spoken to in Tamil. My personal belief system always maintained that one cannot win the hearts and minds of the people by being rough on them. The environment at the time was also not very threatening as the Tamil terrorist groups were few, consisting of a total of three to four dozen cadres. They were not armed with sophisticated weapons as they are today. Most of them were armed with .38 revolvers and a few with .303 or G4 rifles and grenades.

In Gurunagar, we were about to commence the anti-terrorist operations. I started my own intelligence system. There was a small but enthusiastic band of about half a dozen officers from various units and some other ranks posted to me who were available to work independently in small groups, sometimes consisting of only two or three who went out to collect intelligence. I made use of my own soldiers who were very good in Tamil and set them to collect information. There were Tamil and Muslim soldiers as well. Some of the Sinhalese soldiers spoke fluent Tamil. Staff Sergeant Namunudasa spoke all three languages. He was a brilliant soldier as well. The soldiers would pal up with the youth in the area, eat their *dosa* and collect information. When they returned to the camp the information was put together and we worked out what was going on. There were about eight officers and 125 men posted for duties. This group, although small in number, consisted of soldiers mainly from the newly raised Commando Regiment commanded by Major Sunil Pieris (later the first Commanding Officer). Two officers (one now a Major General) provided the expertise to the regular troops in the raids and ambushes. Reliable and timely intelligence supported by an enthusiastic and dedicated staff produced good results without a single casualty. The GSO 1 and staff officers gave daily briefings to all ranks on the intelligence situation, the past and probable future of terrorist activities which created enthusiasm and encouraged team work. The Internal Security Department (ISD) of the police, later re-organized as the National Intelligence Bureau (NIB) had deployed staff to supplement investigations and intelligence. They provided us with the expertise to organize the intelligence data and compile an index. The army intelligence unit of Gurunagar was fortunate to have these experienced ISD/NIB officers. One such pioneer was Mr. T.M.B. Mahath, a quiet unassuming police officer, who later went on to become a Senior Superintendent of Police.

The need for intelligence was mandatory in combating the separatist Tamil terrorist groups and it was necessary to enhance this particular aspect. Had we access to finances – not a mere rupees 150 – high quality intelligence would have been easily available, but the authorities were indifferent. There were many instances when officers' ration money was utilized to 'buy' intelligence due to the lack of funds and 'red tape.' Intelligence must not only be accurate, but as importantly, it has to be timely so that it can be effectively used. Infiltration of intelligence members within the enemy as a 'sleeper' is possible if resources are available as an incentive to compensate for the risk and reprisals. Penetration is made more difficult as the LTTE members belonged to one ethnic group.

However, the highest authorities were not very interested. Col. Dharmapala, Secretary to the Ministry of Defence, was of no use. Once I came rushing down to Colombo to brief the Secretary on some urgent matter and the only response I received, between Col. Dharmapala's cigarette puffs, was an indifferent: "So when are you going back?" Even when he was informed that we had information that 25 LTTE cadres were boldly taking the train from Fort to Talaimannar to take the ferry to India, he took no notice. All he did was puff away on his cigar! I thought that with people like this in positions of power, Sri Lanka will have to suffer in the future. The first batch of 25 trainees for the LTTE was given training in Himchal Pradesh. Ravi Jayewardene, son of President J.R. Jayewardene, says that there is a video available of Indian Prime Minister, Indira Gandhi taking the salute of the first batch of LTTE trainees in India.

Meanwhile, I had conducted an operation named *Operation Round Up*. There were photographs of 35 insurgents which were displayed all over the country in post offices. We managed to round up 27 or 28 of them. The others had fled to India. We sent the arrested cadres under escort to Colombo as instructed. To our surprise and dismay we realized that some of those arrested 'suspects' wanted for bank robberies, highway robberies and murder were returning to Jaffna not under escort but as 'free' citizens. Col. Dharmapala did not have the courtesy to inform me that they were being released. The insurgents returned to Jaffna and the soldiers reported to me "*Un dan hari admabara wela*" (They are now very proud).

The official government policy seemed to be inconsistent and would vary from time to time according to political pressure. This was not the first incident of inconsistency. I also remember that when I informed the Secretary Defence that I had very reliable information that Tamil separatist youth were leaving for various unknown destinations in India via the Bandaranaike International Airport for military training, his reply was not only disappointing but also naïve. His reaction was that these were only a few and would not make any difference to their fighting capability. This was an astonishing reply which had devastating consequences to our country, the repercussions for which we are suffering even today. The appointment of Col. Dharmapala was probably one of the worst decisions taken by President J.R. Jayewardene. Though I had direct access to him, President Jayewardene and Col. Dharmapala had been together for a very long time. If I had gone to the President complaining about Col. Dharmapala, I would have been wasting my time. He would have been nice and polite and told me, "We will try to do something about it." It would have been of no use. Either way, I suppose, it would not have made any difference.

At that time, we had very carefully planned operations which involved a few men including an officer to arrest Tamil terrorists based on very reliable intelligence. Operations were conducted on a low key with no publicity. There were many times when the President would contact my staff on the telephone to release, or inquire about the release of detainees. These occasions were rare but my staff was always ready to reason out with him, which he accepted with great understanding. My staff realized that the President was making the call with the TULF politicians beside him.

During the 1971 insurgency, I had reported directly to Mrs. Sirimavo Bandaranaike. There were immediate responses to my concerns. There was no such office to report to when it came to dealing with Tamil insurgents. At the Security Council, the members were the President, Minister of Defence and his deputy, the Defence Secretary, the three service commanders and the IGP. Subsequently, after the NIB was formed, Director Intelligence also attended the meetings. There were also a few Cabinet Ministers who attended by invitation. The Security Council meetings were usually held at the President's House with the service commanders and the IGP, and the Director National Intelligence giving the initial briefing.

There appeared to be a total lack of continuity in the conduct of operations against the armed Tamil terrorists. This is the result of having no policy on how to eradicate terrorism. This type of ethnic based armed conflict, once ignited due to many reasons, is difficult to eradicate without a firm policy derived from strength and practicability.

When considering the past and present events, this is still a great drawback to successfully end the conflict.

The government really started losing control of the peninsula and the population in Jaffna in the late 1970s and early 1980s. The government should have dealt with problems faced by the Tamil people rather than intimidating them. By 1980/81 Jaffna was slowly sliding into the control of the terrorists. Taxes were not being paid and the army was becoming an alien presence, which did nothing but maintain patrols. This may have been a failure on the part of President Jayewardene. But in fairness to him it must be said that one can be the best President, but to make a proper decision one has to be well briefed. If one has 'yes' men around, one cannot make a proper decision. Col. Dharmapala never made any positive contribution. President Jayewardene had Dharmapala in that position, as he trusted him; the President may have believed that Col. Dharmapala will not orchestrate a coup against him. 'Bull' Weeratunga, Col. Dharmapala and President Jayewardene were all related to each other, so it was a close knit circle.

The District Development Councils (DDC) of 1981 was a measure of devolution to win the hearts and minds of the people of the north. If it was properly implemented, we would not be in this situation today. However, the DDC elections themselves were problematic. The LTTE was determined to create chaos. Yet, the government was firm in its stance to hold the elections. The burning of the Jaffna Public Library took place subsequently.

The people of Jaffna hoped that the DDC would work. They expected a great deal from the DDC. If the system worked, the people in Jaffna would have got what they wanted. The Chairman of the Jaffna DDC was the most senior lawyer in Point Pedro, a well respected man. The Chairman visited my office and invited me for the opening of the DDC as I was the senior most military officer in Jaffna. They wanted a ceremonial opening.

But the DDC experiment was a failure as there was very little forthcoming for the DDC in Jaffna. The Minister in charge of the DDC of Jaffna – U.B. Wijekoon - was unfortunately not committed to his job. Each time I came to Colombo he would ride back with me to Jaffna, work a few hours in the GA's Office, have lunch, take a nap and catch the return flight to Colombo. Many of the DDC Members complained to me that the Minister was of no use. He hardly knew the layout of the land.

The Minister in charge of the DDC in Mullaitivu was a Muslim Minister, Mr. Maharoof, who was no better.

On the completion of my period of service in the army, I sent up my papers of retirement to the Ministry of Defence through the usual service channel, the Commander of the Army. I had completed the maximum period of four years in the rank of Brigadier. But it was not to be. My retirement papers were not accepted. Instead, I was informed by the MOD that I had to meet the President, which I did. He advised me against my retirement and asked me politely to continue for another year. I pointed out to the President and the newly appointed Defence Secretary, Mr. G.V.P. Samarasinghe that my extension would create serious complications to the army in particular and the services in general. The Secretary made a note of my reasons for non-acceptance of extension. As there was no further action, I retired after completing an extra year holding the post of Chief-of-Staff and Operations Commander North and East, at the end of the extended period on 4ᵗʰ February 1983.

The SUN newspaper commented on 18ᵗʰ March 1983 under the title 'Take A Bow, Brigadier' - "The colourful service career of a soldier comes to a close as Brigadier Cyril Ranatunga exchanges his Khaki uniform for civilian attire. For 33 years, Brigadier Ranatunga has been what every serviceman would long to be, an outstanding officer who, to quote his own words, has *enjoyed every moment of his career*... Life was rarely without excitement for the fast rising officer... Appointed Chief-Of-Staff Brigadier Ranatunga in the space of one year set up the northern intelligence headquarters and brought the services unto a level of high preparedness. Although retired from service, one is aware that it is impossible to keep a good horse down, and it is a certainty that his talents would be utilized for a long time to come."

Airport and Aviation Services

I retired from military service on 4th February 1983. I was then offered the appointment of Senior Executive Director of Airport and Aviation Services, Sri Lanka (AASSL). I accepted this offer as I was informed that there was to be a massive development project planned to develop this sector, in keeping with the development programme of our country. I had the experience of working with civilians particularly as the Coordinating Officer of the Kegalle and Anuradhapura Districts during the '71 JVP insurgency and during my nearly 35 years of military service. Aviation, however, was an entirely new field which presented at the same time a formidable challenge. I had to learn the technicalities of aviation and the entire new development project. I was especially fortunate to have in my staff the amiable and knowledgeable Mr. John de Saram. He was technically qualified as a Senior Air Traffic Controller. They were the experts in their own fields of responsibility with whom I was fortunate to work. They soon acquainted me with the technical and other issues of the project in a way I could easily understand. Security was handled by experienced retired SSP Mr. T.M.B. Mahath. I was later appointed Chairman, Airport and Aviation Services, which was a company to handle and coordinate the running of the Airport with the Director, Civil Aviation. Its headquarters were located at Havelock Road, Colombo 5.

The consultants responsible for drawing the master plans for our own aviation services were the Netherlands Airport Consultants (NACO) and the Japan Airport Consultants (JAC), from the countries which were funding the project. The terminal building project was undertaken by a consortium of engineering firms, the MTH consortium consisting of Mitsui and Takanaka. One of the terms of the contract was to provide housing and transport for the consultants and their staff. Housing and transport for the consultants would have cost the government a tidy sum had they been compelled to depend on rented housing in Colombo. The decision to build these facilities on site helped the government financially. On completion they were used for our own officials and staff once the project was completed, and therefore was certainly an investment.

Our own engineering team inclusive of the large maintenance staff had to work very closely and coordinate with the foreign contractors as we were constructing a new airport in the same premises as the existing and only functional airport in the country. This challenge was accomplished and credit for that belongs to the entire staff.

Weekly meetings were held with the consultant engineers of the contractors and our own engineers to coordinate the activities and functioning of the airport 24 hours a day everyday. There were serious operational problems with movement of plant and machinery within the airport whilst complying with the safety precautions of the International Civil Aviation Organizations (ICAO). Any incident, however minor would have had serious consequences including temporary closure of the one and only airport available in the country. I was fortunate to have a highly motivated team, both local and foreign, who worked tirelessly and closely with everyone in the project to produce the desired results.

Aviation was a challenging 24-hour profession with its day-to-day or minute-to-minute problems. These problems and challenges kept me busy and thinking as I met qualified professionals ranging from engineering to security as well as the personal problems of my staff.

The airport development plan had got underway in three development packages costing over Rs. 4,500 million with a three-pronged development project, to be in line with the other developed airports in the region. China was also upgrading its airport operations scheduled for completion within five years including 10 airports, secondary radar and other equipment to increase their services. By August 1985, this programme was gathering momentum. The Rs. 4,500 million project included three packages or aspects. There was only one runway, which was not able to accommodate the demands of the gathering development programmes and tourism industry of the country. A new and a much bigger runway was a priority. First in the programme was the 3,350-metre long, 40-metre wide second runway with adequate utilities comprising of cargo, maintenance and navigational services with a more efficient control tower to handle the increasing traffic.

The existing passenger terminal, which was earlier designed to handle 500 passengers an hour, now processed about 1,200 passengers an hour. However, the new terminal envisaged was designed to cater for 1,650 passengers an hour with far superior services. The three major components of the programme planned in 1985 were scheduled for completion and be fully operational as the utilities and ancillaries package by July 1986. The second runway was scheduled for completion and to be operational by August 1986 and was to be laid out parallel to the old runway and would be used only for taxiing to increase the number of aircraft movements. The new terminal building was planned for departures and the existing terminal building was to be used exclusively for arrivals by August 1987. The existing runway needed heavy repairs and this could not be undertaken until the new runway was complete and commissioned.

The cargo facilities under construction was planned to increase the handling capacity from 28,000 tonnes to 42,000 tonnes annually. This facility would finally be developed into a transhipment centre consisting of complete cold storage facilities. The contractors handling the three projects were Kajima Corporation, Kajima Road and C. Itoh of Japan. The terminal building was constructed by MTH Consortium consisting of Mitsui and Takanaka of Japan, and the Utilities Package by GEC Electricals Project Ltd, the UK.

The new Airport and Aviation Services Complex at Katunayake was inaugurated on 12 November 1988 by the President, who was also the Minister in charge of Aviation. The complex comprised the Terminal Building, Runway, Parallel taxiway, Apron, Cargo Complex, new Navigational Services Complex, Control Tower, new fire Services Complex, Maintenance Facilities, separate VIP facilities for Heads of

State, and facilities for all other VVIPs. A Meteorological office and a Met farm too were planned. The most modern navigational system comprising of a Doppler VOR, ILS, Radar and Cat 2 Lighting had been provided.

The airport was capable of handling 30,000 aircraft movements, 2.7 million passengers and 42,000 tonnes of cargo annually. A total of 17 aircraft of different categories could be accommodated in the International aprons and 1,650 passengers could be handled in the peak hour. There are automated baggage handling systems, checking 'in' counters, modern lounges and waiting facilities, information systems, restaurants, shopping complexes for the passenger needs. There was a well coordinated security system with checking devices to ensure passenger safety.

This development project was undertaken to meet the demands of an open economy and encourage the tourist industry as a foreign exchange earner. New and modern facilities were required to meet the growing demand of the increasing number of passengers moving in and out of this international airport from destinations worldwide. The increase in passengers resulted from the relaxation of foreign exchange regulations, international travel and movement of Sri Lankans to the Middle East for employment.

The movement of passenger traffic, which was 393,000 in 1977 when the government assumed office, increased to 1.2 million in 1987. Air Cargo handled in 1977 increased from 6,200 tonnes to 29,000 tonnes in 1987. The construction of these varied facilities unlike other construction demands, required sophisticated technical and engineering skills in many disciplines such as runway construction, airport lighting systems, terminal building construction, Electronic Radar etc. To meet these technical requirements the government commissioned an international firm of consultants, Messrs Lee Acre and Norr of Canada to draw up the master plan, which was funded by the Canadian International Development Agency (CIDA). The growth rate of the traffic was so rapid that the plan had to be revised in 1981 by a Dutch firm of consultants – Netherlands Airport Consultants Organization (NACO) funded by the Netherlands Government.

It was at the height of this activity that I was summoned by President J.R. Jayewardene and asked to take over the Joint Operations Command (JOC) as the General Officer Commanding. It was, for a soldier, the highest honour bestowed: an honour, which left me with no alternative, but to accept.

I was, to say the least, disappointed to handover and leave a major development project to which I had given total commitment and was keen to see completed. But now the writing was on the wall. The President gave me just 24 hours to decide when I called on him the next day. He was quite firm and had decided for me when he said that he had every right to recall me from the regular reserve to serve the country. I decided to get back into uniform and the serious defence commitments that it entailed, however long it was to be. This change gave my tailor a great deal of work in stitching my uniforms and the army had to provide me with the accoutrement that I required. I bade goodbye to the consultants, the engineers and all my staff and bade farewell to the aviation industry.

The '83 Riots and their Aftermath/ 'Black July'

With the clashes between the terrorists and the Sri Lanka Government forces continuing with no sign of respite, the country entered the year 1983 with no hopes of peace in the near future. In March 1983, the government called for fresh elections for the local government bodies in the whole country and by-elections for 18 seats in Parliament. With the country set for a mini-general election, the terrorists, particularly the LTTE, threatened the parties who contested the elections.

On the morning of 29th April 1983, three candidates contesting the local upcoming elections were killed by the LTTE. These three murders sent shock waves within the Jaffna District and people started fearing for their lives.

Umamaheshwaran had by this time broken away from the LTTE and formed his own terrorist group – PLOTE (People's Liberation Organization of Tamil Eelam). While trying to gain control of Vavuniya, he blasted an air force jeep in Vavuniya on 1st June 1983, killing two air force men. These killings resulted in angry Sinhalese rioting in the country against the Tamils. The rioting started in Vavuniya and within a matter of time, it spread to the whole country; the worst affected areas being Kurunegala and Trincomalee Districts.

On 23rd July '83, a patrol in Jaffna was caught in an explosion, in which one officer and 13 soldiers from the Light Infantry were killed. This incident resulted in the anti-Tamil riots, which changed the course of the entire conflict. The riots occurred due to the mismanagement of the funerals of the slain soldiers. The tragedy could definitely have been avoided if the bodies had been sent to the respective villages, rather than bringing them to Colombo and trying to have a common funeral at the General Cemetery in Kanatte. The authorities should have been receptive to the sensitivities and the request for the bodies to be handed over to the loved ones and empathized with the reaction of the majority after the killing of the soldiers.

Myrtle and I were at Kanatte, when the soldiers were to be buried. As the crowd was becoming unruly I contacted the IGP Rudra Rajasingham and General Atygalle who asked me to immediately visit President Jayewardene and to inform him of the opposition from the crowd. After consultation we decided to call off the burial at Kanatte and to send the bodies to the next of kin. But unfortunately the damage had already been done.

As the news of the killing of the 13 soldiers reached the southern parts of Sri Lanka, the entire population was grief stricken and angry at the turn of events. The news of the killing was taken as a major attack on the Sinhalese race.

The anti-Tamil violence and riots broke out soon after the intended funeral of the 13 soldiers at the General Cemetery in Colombo. Very soon the situation spiralled out of control. Hundreds of men, women and children belonging to the Tamil families were killed, injured, burnt and their houses were looted.

The incentive to riot was indeed a curious one. Those who were rioting had no relationship to the dead. Nobody can still point a finger and clearly state who started the riots and who contributed to the spread of it.

There were theories that the 'thugs' who were going around rioting were armed with electoral lists, to help them in their search for Tamil people. However, this was a time of elections and people had electoral lists with them. The electoral lists were freely available, as I can remember. What I always felt was that once some individual commences a course of action there are a large number of people who capitalize on it for personal gain. Several different people get into the act. There are those who want to loot and some who wanted to get personal revenge etc.

There are suspicions that soldiers amongst many others were involved in spreading the 1983 riots. I am not sure how much of it is accurate as I was a civilian during that time. There may have been a few involved as individuals. My personal experience with the 1983 riots was when I was passing the Wellawatte Spinning and Weaving Mills. It was then that I saw a group of Sinhalese throwing stones at some Tamil houses. At that moment, I temporarily forgot that I was a civilian and had retired from the army.

I shouted at them. They disregarded my protesting. In haste, I rushed to my office which was near by, and at this point some of the 'thugs' assaulted me. Some of my colleagues at the office saw what was going on and promptly rushed to rescue me.

Immediately after the rush of events, back at the office I called Army Commander, 'Bull' Weeratunga and requested a platoon so that I could control the whole of the Havelock Town area. But no soldiers were forthcoming.

The general belief is that the army stood by, while the riots went on. However, it must be pointed out that if the IGP had said that the Police could not cope and requested assistance, the army would have got involved.

By Thursday the riots settled, but a rumour had spread on Friday that the Tigers were attacking Colombo, which unleashed another orgy of violence. It was then that the armed forces sprang into action. Though they were inactive at the beginning of the week, they made sure to be very much active at the latter stages. This was a result of the direct orders being given by the President. The President had been silent during the first few days. Statesmen react differently at times of crisis; some are paralyzed by the sudden turn of events at certain times.

This spate of violence against the Tamils by the Sinhalese resulted in a large number of Tamil refugees, numbering over 65,000, being accommodated in several schools, temples and churches etc. By 1st August 1983, the situation returned to normalcy. The unrest that had taken place did not only shock, but in turn became a watershed event in the ethnic conflict in the battle for an independent state of Tamil Eelam. When the situation returned to normalcy, a total number of 471 people were killed in the racial riots which in turn brought the Tamils, the much sought for international favour.

The riots were the turning point in our conflict. There were a large number of people who were harassed and whose properties were looted and damaged. It was those Tamil people who left Sri Lanka for other countries. In turn, it is those very people who support terrorism from their new countries of domicile.

The flow of Tamil refugees to foreign countries with stories of looting, burning and devastation of property naturally appealed to the international community, creating a powerful lobby against the country to justify separatism. Armed Tamil youth outfits mushroomed with the rapid flow of recruits, helped by the emotions of Tamil aspirations.

The Indian Government, with the furtive idea of gaining hegemony, directly and indirectly supported the destabilization process. The major Tamil armed groups consisting of PLOTE, LTTE, EPRLF, EPDP and EROS had as their final goal, a vision of 'Tamil Desam' or 'Tamil Country' consisting of Tamil Nadu and the Northern and Eastern Provinces of Sri Lanka with Trincomalee as the capital.

The People's Liberation Organization of Tamil Eelam (PLOTE) had a central core trained by the PLO (Palestine Liberation Organization) in the Middle East. The Tamil Eelam Liberation Organization (TELO) was a small well knit outfit. Tamil Eelam Army (TEA), however, was a relatively new and small organization which made a sensation with a Rs. 50 million bank robbery at Kathankudy near Batticaloa. Eelam Revolutionary Organization of Students (EROS) was a London-based body of Trotskyite expatriates. Eelam People's Revolutionary Liberation Front (EPRLF) had pretensions more intellectual than military. Its more significant unit was the General Union of Eelam Students (GUES) which was the combined strength of Tamil Eelam Liberation

Army (TELA) and PLOTE. Their combined strength was around 5,000, out of which only one third was armed. Most organizations were Left oriented and had contacts with other leftist guerrilla organizations all over the world. Both LTTE and PLOTE had central fighting cores trained by the PLO. The LTTE Theoretician Anton Balasingham was once reported to have stated that the LTTE's basic alliance was still with the PLO, but that they maintained active contact with the other groups like the Zimbabwe African People's Union (ZAPU), the Zimbabwe African National Union (ZANU) and the African National Congress (ANC).

The PLO-Tamil alliance was even more marked in the case of PLOTE. Its Chief Uma Maheswaran was in the first batch that was trained in Lebanon in 1978. But after a split with the Tigers, he struck a liaison on his own with the People's Liberation Front for Palestine (PLFP) led by George Habash, which, he claimed, was useful. It was also claimed that the Tamil rebels have also had some contact with the Irish Republican Army (IRA) even though they constantly deny it. High level intelligence men, however, have evidence of the liaison and explain that the rebels' anxiety to deny it was because they did not want Scotland Yard on their tail in the United Kingdom.

The situation, prior to July 1983, was explosive due to internal and external forces playing a role to suit their own agenda. In Tamil Nadu, the popular film idol M.G. Ramachandran supported and competed with 'Mu Kha' or M. Karunanidhi to win votes. New Delhi would wheel and deal to clinch an alliance to form a government. Nedumaran of the DMK was considered the 'godfather' of the LTTE separatists. It was they who helped the armed Tamil groups with finances, equipment, medical facilities, while providing them with a safe haven. They also assisted them with smuggling activities which involved heroin and arms, while at the same time, training the militant cadres, organizing political rallies in their support and finally, accommodating the youth in their residences and apartments and assisting them with state communications and providing them with radio facilities. It was always believed that the senior New Delhi ministers, including the Minister of Defence, reportedly entertained LTTE members and other terrorist group members in their houses.

The Sri Lankan Government had well corroborated and documented intelligence of Indian Government agencies training, providing military hardware to, and financing the Tamil separatist groups in New Delhi and Madras. Our own Intelligence was aware of the Indian Government's Research and Analysis Wing (RAW - the foreign intelligence and covert operations arm) gathering information and of their destabilization work.

Some of this information appeared in the prestigious Indian English magazine "India Today" written by Shekar Gupta and was reproduced by *The Island* on 22nd March 1984. It stated that "...batches led by seasoned guerrillas or retired Indian military officers make for the obscure forests and wastelands along the coast in Ramanathapuram District. There, among the casuarinas, the real training and battle inoculations begins. Their target is Sri Lanka, or more precisely, the northern Tamil majority region. Their objective: "An independent sovereign territory of Tamil Eelam." (Gupta, 1984)

In both geographic and strategic terms, they could not have chosen a better training ground. In the words of the rebel leader: "The region is obscure, people and government sympathetic and our dreamland of Eelam right across the sea, just two hours by motorboat. Could we have found a better place?" In fact, from Point Calimere, Jaffna – the Tamil heartland in Sri Lanka – their destination was just a little over an hour away on a good motorboat. And the rebels had plenty of those as was evident from the regular boat traffic between Jaffna and the Indian coast.

The camp near Kumbakonam, like the ones close to Meenambakkam on the outskirts of Madras, is just one of the dozens set up by the Sri Lankan Tamil insurgents deep inside Tamil Nadu, where new recruits were given an ideological grounding by rebel theoreticians, and elementary lessons in the use of firearms. When the initial lessons were completed, they were split into small batches and sent for advanced training to the coast. Underground and Indian intelligence sources estimated 2,000 armed men, belonging to the various groups of Tamil insurgents, were ready for armed conflict.

M.R. Narayan Swamy says in his book *Tigers of Lanka* published by Vijitha Yapa Publications (p.10): "From September 1983 until India and Sri Lanka signed the accord in July 1987, the RAW trained an estimated 1,200 Tamils in the use of automatic and semi-automatic weapons, self-loading rifles, 84 mm rockets, guerilla war, mountaineering, demolitions and anti-tank warfare. Each training capsule lasted three to four months, and rarely six months. Training was also given separately, on the lines of the army, to 'officers' and 'soldiers'. Select members of EROS, LTTE, EPRLF and ENDLF were also given special training in diving and under-sea sabotage. A limited number of Tamils were hand-picked for intelligence gathering. Some trainees were asked to report exclusively on the movement of ships and other activities in Trincomalee."

Yet another 2,000-3,000 had been trained but were reportedly waiting for arms shipments from 'foreign sources' – the Soviet backed leftist guerrilla groups like the Palestine Liberation Organisation (PLO) and Zimbabwean rebels.

Inside Madras the only thing not visible were the guns. But the city was abound with Sri Lankan Tamil insurgents of numerous denominations running training camps in the Tamil Nadu hinterland and plotting an armed showdown against the Government of Sri Lanka. For the LTTE leaders Madras became the most suitable site to have their headquarters. They could operate from the rooms of legislators' hotels. Rebels from various groups ran regular motorboat ferries between the Indian coast and Jaffna. The Sri Lankan Navy at that time had only six seaworthy gunboats, which generally confined themselves to Trincomalee.

Nothing symbolized the build-up better than the feverish activity in a small house in a corner of the upper middle-class Mahalingapuram locality in Madras. There was no signboard that said anything to the average passer by; but almost everyone around knew that No. 9, Narayana Street, housed the Tamil Information Centre and was run by S. Sivanayagam, the former editor of the *Saturday Review*, the pro-Tamil weekly that the Sri Lanka Government banned in July 1983.

Subsequent to the anti-Tamil riots that occurred in July 1983, the villages around Yan Oya and Aththawetunu Wewa assumed a great importance to the LTTE, as they vigorously activated a programme of 'ethnic cleansing' to evict the Sinhalese and the Muslim communities from villages they considered a part of their 'Tamil Homeland.' The Sinhalese and the Muslims who lived in the adjacent villages to those occupied by the Tamil people had lived in amity for many years until then. It was an uphill task to establish a system to provide security to those villages. The LTTE cadres would hide in the jungles adjoining these villages and swoop in, armed with T56 assault rifles, 'kathi,' knives, swords and all types of weapons, against these defenceless villages and slaughter anyone they could. No lives were spared. These were LTTE tactics to 'blood' their young cadres, which comprised often of conscripted children less than 16 years of age.

To give the villagers confidence, they were armed with 12 bore shot guns and supervised by the local Police. Without constant practice, however, the shot gun was no match for the T-56 assault rifle. The villagers were also trained on the principles of camouflage and the basic drills of fire and movement and this training proved effective in preventing many massacres. Some selected persons were also paid by the government as an incentive and were designated as 'homeguards.' Those 'homeguards' had the experience of watching their crops at night to save them from wild boar and elephants and putting the shot guns to effective use. It was easy to criticize the system and there was misuse. However, it was not humanly possible nor was it practical to deploy soldiers in villages, which in turn would have created more problems.

The disadvantage was the lack of communications between the villages and the Security Forces (SF) /Police to ensure timely preventive action. There were no cellular telephones nor were they provided with radio facilities for the hundreds of villages to maintain instant communications. A rather novel, but practical system was adopted, which was the introduction of sirens to warn their own and other villagers of an impending attack.

By the year 1984, President Jayewardene had decided to increase the size of the army. It was at that period in time, certain alarming events took place including the Oberoi Hotel bomb in 1984, the Madras Airport bomb in the same year and the May 1986 bombing of the Air Lanka Tri Star. The terrorists were subsequently gaining their ground in Jaffna too. The entire army in 1978 consisted of only 496 officers and 8,489 other Ranks. This figure in other words amounted to just two Brigades. It included the services – Medical, Military Police, Service Corps (supplies), Ordinance and the Works Services. The Infantry consisted of just three regular battalions with Reconnaissance, Engineer, Artillery and Signals Regiments. This was hardly sufficient to launch major-scale operations. One may argue that the LTTE and the other Tamil armed groups consisted of less than 1,000 or even less than 500 trained, equipped and experienced fighters. But this 1:10 ratio made the task of fighting against trained armed insurgents/terrorist akin to searching for a needle in a haystack in the dark.

G. Parthasarathy, the special emissary of the Indian Government who visited Sri Lanka, denied that India was training Sri Lankan terrorists. Indian Prime Minister Rajiv Gandhi said that India is only looking after refugees from Sri Lanka, not terrorists.

Though we are an independent nation, increasingly we are coming under the influence of India. Significantly the only link we have with India is with Buddhism, but unfortunately, due to the activities of our politicians, we have had more and more interference by India in our future.

By 1987 the strength of the army had increased to 1,740 officers and 24,913 other ranks. This strength was hardly sufficient where the immediate need was for 'boots' on the ground. Many from the south found it difficult to understand the geography of the Jaffna Peninsula; especially the climate and the vegetation, surrounded by sea, and the inland lagoon system. It is natural that their perceptions were coloured by their own experience in the south.

Some of the action that were taken by the Army were very wrong. There are instances where some Tamil youth who had seen a matinee movie were taken straight from the Cinema to a place where they were asked to drop their trousers, and green paint was applied on their bottoms. In some cases they were asked to shave their heads. This type of behaviour made the Tamil youth rise against us.

Joint Operations Command

To meet the increased threat to national security and the worsening of the ground situation, President J.R. Jayewardene established a new anti-terrorist unit to fight the ever increasing spate of subversive activities: The Joint Operations Command (JOC). Formed on 11 February 1985, the JOC was to co-ordinate the activities of the Sri Lanka Army, Navy and Air Force in counter terrorist operations in the north and east of Sri Lanka. "Bull" Weeratunga was appointed the Head of the JOC and a few months later was appointed the High Commissioner in Canada. I was recalled to active service in 1985 as head of the JOC, succeeding "Bull." I was also promoted from Brigadier to Lieutenant General. I accepted the appointment because the President informed me that the Army Commander, Navy Commander, Air Force Commander and the IGP were willing to work amicably under me. Rather than having the three service commanders and the IGP acting independently, it made more sense to have one coordinating authority to plan operations, find out how much each section could do, and modify plans to suit the resources available. The political leadership until that time perhaps did not realize the problems of coordinating military operations. They did not have a coordinated plan for military operations. It was people like Prof. K.M. de Silva who were actively involved in advising President Jayewardene to set up the JOC.

As the General Officer Commanding, JOC, my staff comprised Brigadier Hamilton Wanasinghe – Principal Staff Officer, Lt. Col. Jayantha – General Staff Officer 1, Major Balagalle who subsequently got promoted to Lieutenant Colonel, Major Sunil Tennakoon, Major Chula Seneviratne, Major Sarath Munasinghe, Lt. Col. Daya Wijesekara, Commander Suraj Munasinghe from the Navy and ASP Jurangpathy, who assisted me from the Police.

A major problem that we had was that as a result of the riots, countries who had earlier sold us arms were not willing to sell equipment to Sri Lanka.

For instance, in the case of a tender awarded to an American company, the armoured cars were approved by the American Government, but they refused to release the turret and the gun. The British Government refused to give spares and ammunition for the armoured cars we had bought before 1983. The Saladin armoured cars were seen in action in Sri Lanka during the 1971 insurgency. The crisis made it impossible to get spares for them. The Indians were not supplying arms or equipment to us. But the Chinese Government did not hesitate to provide all our military requirements in huge quantities including aircraft, T-56 assault rifles, RPGs, naval vessels, vehicles including wheeled workshops, and armour. These were sold to us at a very nominal price, barely covering the cost of production. I have given more details of this under tender procedures in this chapter.

Pakistan was also generous in her support. I met the then President General Zia Ul-huq when he visited the island. He guaranteed to provide all required military hardware to combat the terrorists in whatever quantities that we in the military required. He never spoke of the finances involved or the procedure. I was inquisitive to know the time gap between such a request and delivery. He clasped my hand and gave me his personal telephone numbers and asked me to ring him any time of the day. He also promised that the requirement would arrive by aircraft and be delivered on time. He assured me that the delay will be only the time to load and the flight time from Pakistan to Sri Lanka. This was a tremendous encouragement to all of us.

The West had looked aside in our hour of need, and neither did our immediate neighbour respond positively. China, Pakistan, and Israel were the only nations who were willing to provide military assistance for us in those darkest hours.

The Israelis understood our need well though they did not give us the Dvora attack boats we wanted. The officials looked with suspicion at our request and would not hear of any request regarding the dvoras. Finally Ravi Jayewardene met the Prime Minister, Shimon Peres. When he told him that the terrorists were being trained by the PLO, the Israeli PM said, "So we have 2 things in common, you also have terrorists and they are being trained by the same group we are opposed to. We have a common enemy." He then instructed the authorities to give us what we wanted. That was how we got our first Dvora. He actually released 2 Dvoras. He told Ravi Jayawardene, 'Tell your father that whatever his needs are, will be given.

At the JOC, I made a number of changes to our approach in fighting terrorism. What I firmly believed was that you could not ask the soldiers to be engaged in continuous operations. The moment I was asked to take over, I ensured that all servicemen went through a period of compulsory training, comprised of individual training, and training by Section, Platoon, Company, Battalion and Command Posts. Thus, everybody realized what is expected of him when orders are given. During this period, leave was cancelled. It was rigorous but needless to say, effective!

All training was done in places like Maduru Oya, Minneriya and other large complexes that we took over from the Mahaweli Authority. Through those training programmes, the outlook of the soldiers changed as well. After the training programme they were sent on compulsory leave and requested to report on a stipulated date. Once they returned, another battalion was pulled out for training. The soldiers returned rejuvenated and ready to go into battle.

We also introduced a Tamil language training programme. The conduct of operations and the day-to-day work was made even more difficult and often embarrassing due to the inability of officers and troops to speak in Tamil. Due to this inadequacy, some of the officers including troops were unable to converse with the people, and it is they who mattered most in counter terrorist activities. There was also the problem of soldiers being rude or impolite when speaking, but this occurred due to their being ignorant of the language and also not knowing the customs and traditions of the society in which they worked. The simplest solution was to establish a school to teach the Tamil language to servicemen as well as policemen. This task was also given to the General Staff Officer (GSO) 1 Brigadier Daya Wijesekera. In this endeavour to establish the Tamil School, Minister of National Security Lalith Athulathmudali and Minister of Lands and Irrigation Gamini Dissanayake were most helpful. The buildings for the school were provided by Minister Dissanayake near the Kotmale Dam site. It was the ideal location and there could not have been any other place better located. Minister Athulathmudali provided the resources - finances, books, chairs, desks etc. Each course was for three months and every service including the police, was required to provide 25-30 men to maintain balance. Specific and advanced military training and learning of the Tamil language by the forces were a few areas of our final and strategic plan to crush terrorism. It was compulsory that at all times during the course, the participants should speak only in Tamil.

We were fortunate to have the services of a retired infantry Captain Quarter Master (Q.M.) Morseth, who agreed to take on the responsibility of being the head of the school. He was unfortunately killed during the JVP insurrection of 1988-1990. Teachers had to be proficient in both Sinhalese and Tamil and this we remedied by obtaining them from the Education Department. A syllabus was drawn up after consultation with the Education Department to fulfil our aim – mainly for a soldier to be able to read and converse. The school was established by the GSO 1 within two weeks as ordered and officially 'opened' by the Minister of National Security.

During my years we were able to produce 300 servicemen including policemen whose language skills were most useful during Operation Liberation – One. Servicemen proficient in Tamil also played a useful role at checkpoints and road blocks, which certainly improved the 'image' of the servicemen amongst the general public in the north.

However, this policy to continue teaching the Tamil language was not pursued with the commitment it needed and soon the school lapsed into an institution which consisted of servicemen who had no inclination whatsoever to learn.

A Welfare and Rehabilitation Unit was created with an experienced civilian government official in charge as there was the need to establish a unit to cater to civilian activities; mainly the displaced from all communities due to terrorist and other activities. A retired Engineer Colonel was attached as a liaison officer to work with the military. Today they are two Directorates – the Welfare Directorate and the Directorate of Rehabilitation.

An effort was also made to improve the welfare of troops. Two naval landing vessels and a ship were purchased to transport troops from the north and east to ease congestion and delay in getting to and from home on leave. Minister Lalith Athulathmudali and I visited all the camps and I lived with the troops whenever possible. Activities were organized to celebrate the New Year with prizes provided by the JOC. Back in my office, a crack team of officers drawn from all forces were busy drawing up plans on all areas with the aim of launching effective military operations and support services to ensure the well-being of civilians after such operations.

We were busy re-organizing the whole process of military offensives, coordination efforts, welfare, procurement and replenishment of arms and ammunition, training, medical and setting up of efficient media units.

The importance of guaranteeing human rights when assessing governance in a state was emerging as a decisive factor and it was most applicable to the law enforcement authorities. Although military officers were aware of the principles of human rights, most officers expected this to be confined not to themselves but only to the state as they believed they were not personally answerable. I sent my GSO 1 to attend a course on human rights at St. Remo, Italy. He began work on this aspect of the law of war, and at this stage though the instructions on human rights was demoralising to troops as the LTTE never practiced them, many agreed on their importance and applicability once they realised that operations were not conducted in isolated battlefields, but in areas which were thickly populated.

Arrangements were also made with civilian groups and professionals including Dr. A.T. Ariyaratne, Prof. Nandadasa Kodagoda, Winston Dissanayake, the head of "White Flag," Lieutenant Colonel Anil Amerasekera, community leaders especially in the Colombo District and professional medical staff interested in the work to help in creating an environment of goodwill and understanding among all communities. Dr. Ariyaratne was able to reach the people as his organisation Sarvodaya was an islandwide establishment and he was a pioneer in social work for over four decades. Leaflets with extracts from Buddhist texts, the Holy Bible, the Quran, and Hindu texts selected with the help of the religious leaders were distributed to every soldier to raise their morale and provide spiritual comfort to those manning the 'bunkers'; 'there are no atheists in the bunkers.' It is not wrong to say that there were a few rabble rousers as it is in the rest of society. There were attempts to strengthen religious harmony by encouraging a dialogue with the Roman Catholic priests in Jaffna, Mannar and Colombo in early 1986 in the much revered Madhu Church. After long friendly discussions, the Roman Catholic priests quite rightly observed that any crime, or human rights violation committed by whatever ethnic group should be condemned, but there were a few who believed they had a duty by their people and constantly reminded us "but this is our flock" and as such they had to support them as they were among them. This attitude needed further discussion and understanding.

Intelligence was the priority. Each battalion had an intelligence group. Whenever I went to operational areas, the first thing I did was to meet the commanding officer in that area and get the Intelligence Officer to brief me. This gave me the assurance that the whole system in the battalion was working well. This was the first time in the history of the army that a separate intelligence unit was established. All these officers, except two, were later promoted to Majors General and one to Lieutenant General, this latter being the first commanding officer and DMI of the new Military Intelligence unit who went onto to become Commander of the Army and Chief of Defence staff. A vacancy for a Colonel, General Staff (GSO 1) was created and an experienced officer was appointed. He also was entrusted with additional duties as Director, Psychological Operations ('Psyops'), Propaganda and Media. This was the first instance that such a unit was established in the army. This officer had the advantage of studying the 'files' at the Intelligence Services Department (ISD) (later the National Intelligence Bureau or NIB) and preparing the basis for intelligence work at Gurunagar. A TV station was established at Palally with the help of an individual who worked free, but with great dedication and enthusiasm to beam to the Jaffna Peninsula. The radio station beamed programmes to the north and east, which helped to notify the public when conducting operations, especially when imposing and lifting of curfews, where medical, welfare centres and accommodation for displaced etc. were available. The TV station also telecast programmes to the north and east as the government controlled Rupavahini station at Kokavil established midway between Vavuniya and Mankulam on the Jaffna Road was destroyed by the LTTE, killing the two officers and over 50 troops who provided security.

The most effective means for intelligence was the Long Range Reconnaissance Patrol (LRRP). The LRRP is much talked of today as something novel, introduced during the last decade. This impression has to be corrected. The LRRP based on accurate intelligence yielded good results. We were lucky to have an informant who was the brother-in-law of a 'terrorist' leader (name withheld for security reasons) who provided reliable intelligence to arrest many important terrorist cadres.

The story of one very effective and special LRRP team can be told now. The LRRP was led by the late Captain Suresh Hashim. Some of the details of the plan are withheld to maintain secrecy as they may be of use to the enemy even now. Captain Hashim was a Lieutenant in 1 SLLI when he led a four-member LRRP into the jungles many miles south of Trincomalee. They were dropped ashore by boat and found their way in unfamiliar terrain in one and a half days to the ambush site. They lay in ambush for three days and were rewarded with the target – 'Ganesh' - the Trincomalee LTTE Leader and his accomplice.

They escaped under heavy fire into a waiting helicopter on call in the vicinity. What was probably more remarkable was that they brought with them the bodies. Captain Hashim was an exception, at times ill-disciplined but was daring and hardly put off by danger. He was often seen confidently lighting a cigarette under enemy fire much to his own amusement, but not to his nervous comrades. There was only one way to keep him out of trouble and that was to keep him occupied under a strong but sympathetic leader in whom he had confidence.

Procurement for the armed service was given publicity as never before, which in turn demoralized the military and the general public. A brief account of the procedures practiced by the JOC at this point will be appropriate. The entire procedure was handled by Mr. Nimal Jayawardene, as the President of the Procurement Committee along with senior representatives from the armed services appointed by the Service Chiefs. This practice was continued until the latter stages, even when I became the Secretary Defence, Ministry of Defence, with Brigadier Granville Elapatha, the former Director-Budget, Army Headquarters as the MOD representative.

The entire Committee attended only if there was the need to do so and requests for military hardware were tabled and discussed by the committee which I attended as GOC, JOC as it was the service chiefs who executed my operational requirement. Upon agreement on the type and capability of the equipment, the usual Tender Board procedure was adopted with the calling for public tenders to purchase equipment for the Armoured Corps to replace the World War II vintage Daimler and Saladin Armoured cars. Those vehicles were entirely dependent on the United Kingdom for the supply of ammunition, spare parts and accessories which we did not receive due to pressure being exerted from the Tamil community and human rights activists, who were alleging that the military were employed in 'genocide' against the Tamil people. Neither did the US nor the NATO countries agree to supply these spares, which were essential. The Commanding Officers of Armoured Corps recommended and suggested that the Cadillac Gage armoured car and the tender be awarded to the agent based in Singapore.

My position as the GOC resulted in my adoption of the policy that no arms supplier could meet me. However, many arms suppliers did use their initiative to try and arrange discussions. They even resorted to contacting my two sons, without any success in spite of these repeated efforts.

The final tender board suggested two suppliers for Cadillac Gage and Urutur, as two reliable armoured cars to compete for the tender. But Cadillac finally won the deal – a deal worth Rs. 750 million, which resulted in representatives from the Armoured Corps visiting Singapore and Belgium to assess the vehicles for performance.

The President was keen to purchase them as early as possible, but after almost a year he summoned me so as to inquire into the cause of delay. I, as Chairman of the Board, summoned the representatives of Cadillac from Singapore who in turn stated that though the deal was approved by the American Government, only six Cadillac gage Armoured cars could be supplied immediately without the main armament and turret. I felt like using that agent for target practice. What arrogance. What hypocrisy. These are the people who are now preaching to us. We were not asking for charity; we were paying for them.

The Indians are now talking about Sri Lanka turning to Pakistan and China for supplies, but hide the fact that we were forced to do as they did not help us. When we asked for arms to defend Jaffna in the late nineties they offered boats to evacuate our troops!

What do we do when arms supplies are cut off? Maybe we did possess a little bit of luck! Fortunately, the Chinese Foreign Minister and his representatives were in the country at the time. As a last measure, we made the request for China to provide us with the armoured cars. He asked for enough time, which would enable him to consult his government. Within 24 hours China agreed to supply not only the armoured cars but also the tanks and whatever quantities of the T56 assault rifles and ammunition, grenades and explosives we required. The rifles replaced the entire stock of the Self Loading Rifles (SLR) supplied by India and Pakistan since the '71 JVP insurgency. China also agreed to supply the mortars, artillery pieces, gun towing vehicles, self-propelled maintenance workshop vehicles, ammunition transporters, half tonne trucks, four tonne trucks, water bowsers, mines etc.

The problem of procurement was a sensitive issue. This was because it involved public funds and the public interest generated was particularly due to the huge amounts of finances involved in the transactions.

Until then, the military had not been involved in making purchases on the scale now required, due to the violent escalation of the armed conflict and the increase in the Defence Budget, especially for the army. Many parties were interested and secured tenders for the supply of arms and military hardware which included small arms, heavy weapons and weapon systems, aircraft, including helicopters, flak jackets, ships, fast attack craft, vehicles of all varieties etc. There were as many competitors as there were arms dealers as stakeholders to give media publicity against competitors. There was also professional competition at the highest levels as many did not miss the opportunity to harm colleagues for their own advancement, as many arms dealers had direct contacts with military officials involved in the purchasing process and also due to the fact that retired senior officers who had previous experience in purchasing military hardware were employed by the competitors hoping to influence the deals.

The government was aware of the situation. The defence establishment, including the President, Prime Minister and State Minister Mr. Ranjan Wijeratne, was keen to adopt the correct procedures. The usual selection and proposals for the purchase of military hardware were prepared by the service commanders according to the regulations and procedures which were necessary to determine suitability of equipment and other factors pertaining to performance. There was an additional safeguard in the form of a Special Cabinet Sub-Committee to place tenders before they were put up to the cabinet by the Minister of Defence.

No purchases were made without a firm recommendation of the Service Commanders or the Inspector General of Police. There were certain instances when tenders were not called, as in the case of the Y-8 aircraft which was manufactured by the C.A.T.I.C. in China. Two of them were purchased, of which one was lost in a mishap with its entire crew on board. The replacement for this aircraft was negotiated by the Commander of the Air Force and his team of technical officers. Arrangements were made to purchase it on a long-term payment scheme.

Many are indeed aware that the firm NORINCO is a Chinese Government Organization, which has been our most dependable supplier for years. At a time when all other manufacturing countries of military hardware refused sales and end user licences to Sri Lanka, it must be reiterated that if not for NORINCO, the armed conflict had every reason to end in sheer disaster. There was absolutely no interference in the cancellation of the previous tenders and NORINCO supplied us with our needs before other organizations had the opportunity to respond to the public tender procedure.

Selection of military hardware has always been a matter for the Tender Board and the Cabinet Sub-Committee and must be finally approved by the Cabinet of Ministers. There has never been a deviation from this procedure. Even at times of severe crisis and special circumstances, the Tender Board had met and made recommendations to the Cabinet Sub-Committee and the Cabinet.

It was agreed to permit the recommendation of the Commander of the Air Force to purchase Tucano (Argentinean) aircraft, evaluated to be superior to the Sia Machetti (Italian) which were being used at that point. The President, however, disagreed and insisted that the tender be re-advertised, after which a team of senior air force officers, including technical officers proceeded to Argentina and Italy to evaluate both sets of aircraft. All delegations arrived with the concurrence of the government and their proposals were equally evaluated and assessed. In the case of a credit package, it had to be evaluated by the Finance Ministry as the Minister of Defence had no authority to negotiate financial packages or transactions. The strict adherence to the accepted Tender Board procedures not only helped to maintain transparency, but also helped to encourage confidence in the procedures that were adopted by the government in the arms deals.

These procedures can still be scrutinized by any government official instead of putting forth criticism from time to time which only results in demoralizing the military and the people of this country.

There were a few incidents which made an operation of a larger-scale mandatory. In April 1987, the LTTE engaged in a series of attacks against military and civilian targets. The LTTE had captured eight soldiers and demanded the release of 25 LTTE members in government custody to begin negotiations. They also demanded that the fuel embargo imposed by the government be lifted immediately and accused the government of bombing the Jaffna Hospital. It later turned out that the LTTE was responsible for the incident.

Around 1730 hours, during the rush hour after work in the city of Colombo, the LTTE detonated a powerful bomb killing over 106 civilians and injuring over 200 at the Pettah Bus Stand. It was obvious that the LTTE expected a severe backlash similar to that which followed the killing of the 13 soldiers in the Jaffna Peninsula on 23rd July 1983, but they were disappointed in that expectation as no reaction ensued.

Following the LTTE rejection of the 19th December proposals of the government, their activities showed that they were preparing for armed conflict. There were also statements by LTTE spokesman Balasubramanium Canagaretnam alias Raheem that they were preparing for a defensive battle. They, however, indicated that they would resume talks in principle based on the December 19 proposals, as suggested by Minister Thondaman. The cabinet had almost agreed to lift the fuel restrictions, but it was torpedoed by the LTTE massacring innocent civilians. A unilateral truce was to commence on 11th April. But the LTTE massacred 129 civilians including men, women, and children of all age groups in the village of Kitulutuwa.

The LTTE also simultaneously attacked 18 other Sinhalese villages. These incidents were followed by the Colombo truck bomb explosion at the Central Bank, which caused massive destruction and carnage. Curfew was immediately imposed mainly to prevent another anti-Tamil riot, which could have been triggered by certain groups, given the escalating violence.

Massacres of Sinhalese villagers in the LTTE 'ethnic cleansing' programme continued to frighten innocent villagers who had lived in those places for generations. Conducting military operations haphazardly as a fire fighting exercise was an exercise in manpower, wastage and resources yielding no permanent results or solutions. The urgent need was to eliminate the terrorist 'bases' so that they could not conduct these raids in the villages in order to achieve their aim of 'ethnic cleansing.'

Activities Preceding 'Operation Liberation – One'

I had retired in 1982 and was not directly involved in military operations for nearly three years. But I was perhaps compensated with my civilian experience as head of the Airport and Aviation Authority where there was the opportunity to interact with qualified and capable civilians in the vast area of Airport and Aviation work. Moreover, it was both similar and at the same time unlike the military, which was what I was used to. It was helpful in the sense that like in the military, quick solutions to problems were required in this civilian environment.

On assuming the appointment at JOC (Joint Operations Command) after General Weeratunga, more troops and equipment would have been helpful. However, we realized that this was not practical. At the same time there was an urgency to bring the armed conflict to a successful conclusion. There was a steady erosion of the country's economic resources and a fear which was not conducive to foreign and local investment. I had to be mindful of the unfortunate consequences of the '83 communal riots, which I had experienced. The Tamil community had raised this matter at international levels and any operations I had in mind had to be sensitive not to arouse sensitivities for repetition.

Another matter which needed urgent attention was to obtain the experience of civilians as well as their participation before and after the conduct of JOC operations. My civilian experience stood me in good stead. There were question of the poor 'image' of troops and the law enforcement authorities due to various allegations. Human rights violations, missing persons, the neglect of the displaced, medical requirements, food distribution and many other areas required immediate solutions. These were top priorities which needed urgent attention.

The Security Forces (SF) had conducted operations in the Trincomalee, Kilinochchi, Mannar, Mullaitivu and Vavuniya Districts and in the Northern and Eastern Provinces attacking hideouts, jungle training camps and 'flushing out' and 'pushing' the LTTE to the Peninsula. A series of discussions were held at all levels at the JOC and although disagreement existed between officers and ministers, the final decision remained my responsibility.

During these preparatory stages, localized offensives against the terrorists were being conducted with a great deal of success. All operations were conducted in a professional manner with army, navy, air force and police contributing effectively. All area commanders in the troubled areas were handpicked efficient officers who commanded the respect of the soldiers.

One of the first successful major operations after I assumed duties at the JOC was conducted in Trincomalee, codenamed Ranthambili (Golden King Coconuts) in 1986. A media report described this as "The government's single major breakthrough in the battle against terrorism... when the security forces overran a terrorist base camp in the Trincomalee District."

Nearly 33 terrorists were reported killed and 97 were arrested and the area was brought under government control. The terrorist headquarters at that time was located in the popular tourist resort of Nilaveli, equipped with field telephones and an elaborate bunker/trench system. The troops recovered barrels of petrol and trucks hidden in the thick undergrowth.

Colombo was always treated as the centre for the administration. Command control, operational planning maintaining operational maps were all done in the Joint Operation Command office. The joint command consisted of the Commanders of the Army, Navy, Air Force and Police. They were kings in their respective offices but treated as equals in the office. The operations office had a huge map of Sri Lanka on the wall and it was updated every few minutes. Not everyone would go into the operation room as the map had markers to indicate the position of the troops. There were duty officers to make sure that it was updated on a 24 hour basis and no outsiders were allowed to go into this room.

Once, coming into office I walked into the command room to see Lalith Athulathmudali and 2 strangers. I was very angry. Who had asked these outsiders to come into the room? I slammed the door and went to my office. A few minutes later Lalith came and apologised and said that he did not know there were rules that outsiders should not be allowed into the room. We shook hands and that was the end of the matter. And never again did Lalith bring in outsiders, nor do I to this day know who the two strangers were.

Vadamarachchi: 'Operation Liberation – One'

There were many considerations for the selection of Vadamarachchi. It was selected after hours of meticulous planning and a lot of afterthought. Since assuming duties as General Officer Commanding of the JOC, many operations were conducted in various areas and the war was fought on many fronts with several groups of terrorists, ranging from EPRLF, PLOTE, LTTE, TELO and EROS. Each group employed different guerrilla tactics with the common aim of becoming the supreme group with a popular tag in calling themselves the liberators of the suffering Tamil population of the north and east of Sri Lanka.

All the localized operations were carefully planned with the army, navy, air force and the police, and subsequently, had the desired results. I was fortunate to have a crack team of officers in the forces who undertook these operations with great commitment and valour. The intelligence unit which was formed during my days in Gurunagar played a vital role in all these operations. With most terrorist groups becoming weak after the security forces launched successful operations, the remaining cadres joined the emerging group, the LTTE and the people who opted not to join, were brutally murdered by the LTTE. We, in the JOC saw what was happening in a completely different perspective. It was clear that the LTTE would soon be the sole terrorist group, and that the security forces would have to deal with them consequently.

The requirement of a full-scale war aiming at the leaders of the LTTE, giving them a crippling blow was in my mind. I kept on thinking about the various aspects for a couple of days without letting any of my inner circle of commanders and the intelligence officers know, as I had to be convinced in my own mind that an operation of this magnitude needed to be carefully thought about, as civilian casualties, security forces casualties, the reaction of the international community, the impending Indian support for the LTTE, arms and ammunition were all of utmost importance. Everything needed careful and precise planning. During those first few days, my mind was racked with questions and I was crippled with doubt and uncertainty. Some of the officers working closely with me noticed that I was preoccupied and it later came to be known that after many discussions amongst them, they had decided to confront me.

This discussion did take place. Their confrontation had the desired results – I proceeded to tell Brig. Denzil Kobbekaduwa, Col. Lionel Balagalle and Lt. Col. Sunil Tennakoon my idea. I immediately saw Denzil's mind drawing up battle plans. Lionel and Sunil, the most senior intelligence officers with a tremendous track record, were in deep thought. They left my room with a promise that only the four of us will know what was going on in my mind.

Denzil was very keenly involved and wanted any vital information conveyed to him. Once, when a top terrorist was apprehended, a soldier rushed to his quarters to tell Denzil the news. Denzil, who was shaving in the bathroom, walked out. The soldier got the shock of his life to see a completely naked Denzil, who had been so excited by the news that he forgot to wrap a towel round himself. He could well have told the soldier, as in the famous case involving Winston Churchill in the buff, "Sri Lanka has nothing to hide."

With tremendous pressure on the Sri Lankan Government from the international community to solve the ethnic problem by negotiations, and the Sri Lankan forces being unfairly accused of human rights violations, President JRJ requested that I keep him informed of the real situation on a regular basis at the time of my appointment. I was authorized to drive into his residence 'Braemar' anytime in the evening to brief him about the situation at the time. However, I did feel that to inform the President of an idea of an operation of this magnitude was premature.

In the meantime, plans were underway for 'Operation Short Shift'. This was an offensive carried out mainly by the Sri Lanka Navy with the Air Force to get food supplies to the besieged Jaffna Fort as light machine gun fire by the LTTE had hampered air operations hitherto carried out. I convened a meeting of the commanders of the three forces, the IGP, a few selected senior officers and my intelligence staff to discuss the plan for an all out war. I must reiterate that I had total confidence in the initial team I selected for this purpose. I was fortunate to have a team of such professional officers, and discussions were only limited to the operations room in the JOC headquarters.

Intelligence units in the north were mobilized in full-scale to gather information regarding the LTTE hierarchy. Other intelligence teams worked on civilian population, smuggling operations, LTTE arms and ammunition procurement systems. With credible information from all intelligence units, who at great risk to their lives obtained vital intelligence, helped us to dot the map for the operations. It was decided to launch the offensive in the Vadamarachchi area covering VVT, which is at the northern tip of the Peninsula. This incidentally happened to be the birthplace of the LTTE Leader and his senior cadres. The heart of the Tamil separatism and its military arm of terrorism originated and was kept alive in VVT.

It was no co-incidence that it was in the well-known smuggler's house in VVT that the three major Tamil political parties, who until that time opposed each other at elections, met. The parties were Tamil Congress (TC), Federal Party (FP) and the Ceylon Workers' Congress (CWC). They unanimously signed the agreement uniting to become the Tamil United Front, which later went on to become the Tamil United Liberation Front (TULF) with the joint understanding that a 'Tamil' will not contest another 'Tamil.' Other than VVT being a base for separatists, it had been transformed into a formidable defence position with barbed wire entanglements, trenches, strong points, mines, improvised explosive devices (IEDs), anti-personnel mines, heavy and light machine gun nests manned by their best Indian and

PLO trained cadres. VVT was also thickly populated with a warren of houses, by-paths and by-lanes adjacent to the main road running by the sea, creating problems for conducting operations. The main Point Pedro Road ran parallel to the coast and the entire population consisted of people from the closely-knit fisher caste; a caste which was not considered to be at the top of the Tamil social structure. The livelihood of the people had been fishing and smuggling from time immemorial. Many Hindu *kovils* dotted the land and Hindu festivals were celebrated with great enthusiasm. A special feature was that many houses of the rich, the famous and the notorious had canals built right into their houses from the sea which were used for smuggling. A military assault would therefore have easily caused the displacement of thousands of people.

The battle plans were now being drawn. It was necessary to deceive the LTTE and the media (local and foreign) about our plan as this would have given the enemy time to prepare and replenish stocks of explosives in the area and to avoid international pressure on the Government of Sri Lanka. As such, a unanimous decision was made not to mention Vadamarachchi in any operational plan, but to replace it with a general term, Jaffna. This was only a precaution. Planning sessions with different teams consisting of officers from all forces went on for many weeks. When the planning process and selecting the ground commanders for the operation was finalized, I visited Braemar and spoke of my plan with the President. He became very quiet and went into deep thought. With a sudden smile on his face, he offered me a Cuban cigar and a brandy which I had to politely refuse as the operations team was waiting for my return. Instead I was given biscuits and tea whilst we discussed the possible repercussions. Finally he nodded and said, "You can flatten Jaffna, if this menace can be eradicated, and I will build a new Jaffna!"

With this information, I went back to the waiting officers of the operations room of the headquarters. We were just completing elaborate plans which had been meticulously worked out by expert teams for media, psyops (psychological operations), battle commanders, battle objectives, troop requirements, heavy armour, arms and ammunition, transportation, casualty evacuation, logistics, communications, medical rehabilitation and welfare, amongst many others. Sri Lankan forces were preparing for its first divisional sized offensive in its history.

Special teams from the army, navy, air force and the police worked round the clock on logistical issues, which was a monumental task. Battle commanders were selected. Sri Lanka had the luxury of having three of the best battle hardened officers in Brig. Denzil Kobbekaduwa, Col. Wijaya Wimalaratne and Brig. Gerry De Silva. I was confident that the mention of the three names amongst the officers and troops would have boosted the morale and prepared the forces mentally for the biggest battle we were about to launch. Needless to say all the officers selected for the launch of 'Operation Liberation' were of very high commitment and valour. Their love for the motherland was seen on their faces when I first briefed them of the impending battle. The three brigades commanded by the veterans of many battles were to undertake different roles. An imaginary line was mapped across Vadamarachchi area and Col. Wijaya Wimalaratne was entrusted in launching the operation from the northern theatre of Vadamarachchi. Brig. Denzil Kobbekaduwa's brigade was scheduled to proceed north from the south of Vadamarachchi, strangling the LTTE and trapping them within the Vadamarachchi area. Brig. Gerry de Silva's brigade had multi-task operations ranging from VVT, Jaffna Fort and the general Jaffna Town area. Each of the Brigade Commanders had a detailed plan of the objectives and a mobile operations room that was in touch with each other, and main operations centre in the Palaly Army Camp from where all activities were to be coordinated.

Mr. Lalith Athulathmudali – Minister of National Security – although not from a military background, understood the plan and the execution in total. Mr. Athulathmudali spent a long time in Palaly

Army Base during the operations and tackled the sensitive issues with remarkable efficiency.

The Vadamarachchi operation was kept as a top secret among the officers and Lalith Athulathmudali was told about the planned attack a few hours before it began, or to be precise, the last day before the attack. It was not a question of trust. I got permission from President Jayewardene for the operation, and to inform only my immediate staff and 3 service commanders.

Lalith Athulathmudali wanted me to flatten Vadamarachchi and even wanted to arrange for the bulldozers to do the job. I refused to do it and said, 'Not a single house will be destroyed by dozer while I am in command.'

I had a close relationship with Lalith, and even after he had his problems with Premadasa and formed his own party, I assisted him in security. I had no authority to give official security to him but I knew he was under threat and tried to help. Once his security men were suspicious of my men in civil who were waiting around and reported it to Lalith. My men then had to reveal who they were and that they had been sent by me. Lalith phoned me and thanked me. It was very touching, but unfortunately he was killed at a rally in Kirulapone.

The forces were blessed with the presence of prominent civil doctors who volunteered to work in Palaly to treat the wounded during the Operation Liberation: Dr. Roshnara Gunaratne, Dr. Rohan Pethiyagoda, Dr. Michael Abeyratne, the late Dr. Mrs. Kamalika Abeyratne, Dr. Narendra Wijemanne and Dr. Mrs. Hiranthi Wijemanne were some who worked along with the army doctors in the Palaly Army Hospital. Mr. Rohan Jinasena and his mechanical minded brothers of the Jinasena Group were ever willing to come to the assistance of the army mechanical engineers whenever required. In hindsight, I recall, the Forward Headquarters of the JOC based in the Palaly Military Base was a hive of activity, just like a 'bee hive', where everyone was putting the final touches to the operation.

108

Before 'D' day, I had the final briefing with the three ground commanders and the intelligence team to ensure that the entire plan was in place. Thus Operation Liberation was launched on 26th November 1987.

Among those who participated in the Vadamarachchi operation were Sarath Fonseka (now the Army Commander) and Gotabhaya Rajapakse (now the Defence Secretary).

'Liberation – 1' was electrifying, and is best brought back to memory through a letter written by Lieutenant Commander Lucky Dissanayake to his wife, Cynthia, which was received by her after Operation Liberation began:

"The situation here is unbelievable. It is the preparation for war on a scale I have only seen in films. There are about 5,000 troops, armoured cars, armoured vehicles, artillery etc. Yesterday the entire brigade had assembled for review by the General on the adjoining airfield. About 10-15 times bigger than any Independence Day parade, with fighter planes, helicopters, transport planes etc. As the troops in their full battle dress, camouflage, kept marching into the grounds, we in the hospital realized that this was history in the making. This was the first time ever in the history of Sri Lanka that a number of Brigades had assembled. The sight of all of these young boys (18-20) all looking trim, loaded with equipment made us feel proud. The cream of the army was here. The General (GOC of JOC) addressed the officers before the battle. It was reminiscent of the likes of General Patton. He ended his address saying that he assembled here, the best medical teams in the country and that they had nothing to worry. He repeated this at the Commanders' conference too. I have gone with him to some of the smaller companies and feel proud to serve with him and his team. Work-wise, so far we have dealt with accidental explosions and misfires – but no doubt, we will be stretched soon. Tell the boys (sons) that I am taking part in history and that perhaps one day they too may have the same opportunity... The air is full of expectations, but the morale is high. I wish you could have been here, You would be proud of our services. Pray for me and for an easy victory. God Bless!"

The Lieutenant Commander was a skilled cancer surgeon with a wonderful sense of humour and a strong sense of dedication for his fellow men, soldier or civilian. He was also the son of a former Inspector General of Police S.A. Dissanayake. He loved his profession, but his heart was in the services. Many years later he was drowned in the sea, which for me was always a tragedy.

As Operation Liberation got into full swing, my ground commanders were reporting successful completion of tasks which were meticulously planned, executed and monitored. The military machinery got into top gear and weeks of planning every aspect was now beginning to yield results.

We were confident that by now the Tigers were running out of supplies, arms and ammunition and would start crying for international help. For the first time the LTTE announced that their demand for a separate state was negotiable. Sri Lankan military intelligence was a hive of activity. It was just another 10 days of intense fighting that would have killed or captured the Tiger hierarchy.

Even at the planning stages of Operation Liberation a great deal of thought was given to Indian involvement. One thing that haunted me was how Mrs. Indira Gandhi initially supported the rebel groups by training different groups in various parts of India. M.G. Ramachandran, then Chief Minister of Tamil Nadu, was a strong supporter of the so-called Tamil cause and the involvement of the Indian intelligence agencies with various Tamil groups.

M.R. Narayan Swamy says in his book *Prabhakaran: Inside an Elusive Mind* (published by Vijitha Yapa Publications) what happened when MGR met the LTTE group: "MGR (pp. 106,107) was already ill by then and presented a pitiable figure, saliva dripping from the left corner of his mouth. His ability to speak was greatly impaired after he had suffered a stroke. He kept a pile of small towels by his side from which he would pick one, wipe the saliva and dump it into a box, while aides kept a steady supply of fresh towels.

"The LTTE delegation presented a brief history of the guerrilla group and went on to highlight the atrocities being committed on Tamil civilians in Sri Lanka by the security forces. The LTTE members explained that while they sincerely appreciated the support and sympathy of the governments and people of India and Tamil Nadu, there was an urgent need for monetary assistance. Would MGR do something for them?

"MGR sat impassively on a chair, his dark glasses hiding his eyes and a fur cap covering his bald head. As the LTTE's Balasingham broached the subject of funds, MGR listened patiently and asked him how much money LTTE was expecting from him. Taken aback, Balasingham replied they were willing to accept whatever MGR was gracious enough to grant. MGR suddenly raised two fingers of his right hand in a V sign and asked in Tamil: Will two be enough?

"Assuming he was referring to 200,000 rupees, the LTTE members nodded, happy that such a large sum was being offered at their very first meeting. MGR had actually meant a massive two crores, or 20 million Indian rupees! When the cash was actually placed, LTTE representatives were dumbfounded. They had never seen such a large amount of money. The amount was so huge that MGR was politely informed that the LTTE would prefer to accept it in instalments. The chief minister had no problem.

"When the LTTE delegation broke the news of the financial windfall to Prabhakaran, he was equally stunned. Prabhakaran decided to call on MGR at the earliest to thank him for his support. When the two met, they hit it off right away.

"One of the early photographs of the two together showed the LTTE chief, with close-cropped hair, standing reverentially before the chief minister. Prabhakaran never forgot the magnanimity displayed by MGR and became his instant admirer. So much so that throughout his near four-year stay in Tamil Nadu, and despite requests from friends, he refused to meet or even greet MGR's arch political rival, Karunanidhi. When Karunanidhi decided to give away 25,000 Indian rupees to each Sri Lankan Tamil guerrilla group, the LTTE declined. And unlike leaders of EROS, EPRLF and TELO, Prabhakaran refused to pose for photographs with Karunanidhi, who prided himself as the unchallenged leader of Tamils around the world. This pleased MGR no end and further cemented the bond between the two."

There is no doubt in my mind that Indian policy makers during the early years of the conflict had ulterior motives in getting involved in the conflict through training and supplying of arms to terrorists. As we went into the final stage of planning this operation, we had credible information that RAW (Research and Analysis Wing) was involved in arming the terrorists. However, the Indian intelligence agencies and the Government of India kept denying this publicly. With all the backing the terrorists received from India and the money pouring into LTTE coffers from Tamil Nadu, we knew that India will not allow the Sri Lankan forces to completely crush the LTTE, if the operation dragged on for too long.

We were also aware of the sea route to Tamil Nadu, which the Tigers used at will to ferry and treat the injured cadres. With limited resources, the Sri Lankan Navy did a remarkable job as per the operational plan in blocking Tigers plying on this sea route. Our signals unit monitoring Tiger communications intercepted urgent pleas going to the cadres in Tamil Nadu to take up the issue of saving them from annihilation with the Tamil Nadu Chief Minister. One common excuse used was the killing of the innocent Tamil civilians. During the operation in VVT, I often conferred with the ground commanders in their mobile headquarters in the battle fields and the urgency of completing the task was discussed at length. Our ground intelligence received vital information which confirmed that the Tiger hierarchy was getting cornered. The morale of the ground troops was high and we were sensing a prize catch when I was called by the President to be told that the Indian Government was exerting pressure on the Sri Lankan Government to halt the offensive and relief supplies for the Tamils in the north will be sent from Tamil Nadu on hired boats.

President Jayewardene and Mr. Lalith Athulathmudali were furious. We took a decision to block the relief supplies and send them back saying that we can manage our own affairs. This was a clear indication of India's interference in Sri Lankan affairs. Strong protests were lodged in the Indian High Commission and the newspapers carried detailed information regarding the unsolicited help from India. It is sad that except Pakistan and China, all other foreign missions chose to ignore this. The flotilla of Indian boats decided not to proceed towards Sri Lanka when our Navy confronted them within sight of our territorial waters and said they will be fired on if they come within our waters.

The following day, President Jayewardene called me and ordered a temporary halt of the Operation as the Indian Air Force was bringing in food supplies. When I protested, a visibly angry President retorted that we could not fight India. I was given a Presidential order and I had to carry out the instructions. India is one party to this internal conflict who should take the majority of the blame. They trained, armed and provided financial assistance to the terrorists and was now instrumental in halting an operation that would have wiped out the LTTE menace.

International leaders and so-called superpowers chose to ignore this blatant interference, which I call hypocrisy. A nation like ours was too small to benefit the bigger players in the world to get involved irrespective of human duty. I was thoroughly dejected and wondered how I could give instructions to stop the offensive, which was nearing completion. The troops on the ground who were ready to sacrifice their lives to liberate our country from the terrorist menace would react in different ways. The instructions I received gave me approximately two hours to bring the offensive to a halt. I had to visit the troops on the battlefield and break the news. For the first time, I saw the disappointment in their faces. Some found it difficult to accept and even questioned their company commanders how India could do such things.

Finally, Operation Liberation was called off.

Indian intrusion and arrival of IPKF

After blocking the Indian boats with so-called relief, we in the military knew there was more to come. After all, India had trained, armed and financed the separatist groups with the intention of getting fully involved in the internal affairs of Sri Lanka. I was in Palaly Military Base when I received a telephone call on the secure line from the Commander in Chief, President J.R. Jayewardene. The conversation was very brief when he said, "Cyril, Indian aircraft will arrive into our air space in Jaffna Peninsula. Do not interfere." This air drop was scheduled for 4th June 1987 between 3:00 and 5:00 p.m. I proceeded to the control tower with my commanders and watched the arriving Indian aircraft with sheer frustration.

It clearly showed the hand of India and the intensity of Indian intents on our country. It dawned on me that such high handed autocratic decisions were not taken overnight, but well in advance. The final goal may have been to achieve a sense of hegemony in the region. As clichéd as the next line may sound, I will never forget and will not forgive India to my dying day. My disillusionment knew no bounds.

Suddenly, Indian High Commissioner Mr. J.N. Dixit, the worst High Commissioner India has ever sent who was a 'know-it-all' with his head in the air, commenced making statements that he wanted to save Sri Lanka and it was this concern that forced India to pressurize Sri Lanka to stop the military actions. The Indian High Commissioner had diplomatic privileges of inviting local and foreign diplomats and giving the Indian version of the intrusion. The Indian Government was insisting on mediation. Pakistan was refusing to get directly involved due to Indian intervention, but publicly claimed that it was purely an internal affair of Sri Lanka.

When President Jayewardene asked Dixit how Rajiv Gandhi (Indian Prime-Minister) would react if Sri Lanka did not want Indian help or involvement, he responded, "You will forgive me for saying this, Mr. President. The unpredictable consequences may be LTTE asking for operational support from Tamil Nadu and it might end up with the break up of Sri Lanka. Sri Lanka may not remain a united country." The President shot back: "Mr. Dixit, true we are a small country, but I want you to know that I will not succumb to terrorist violence regardless of what you are saying. Please also note that this violence has been and is being supported by your government and your country." Dixit continued unabashedly: "Government forces were strategically and tactically dominating the Vadamarachchi area. The Sri Lankan Government should take note of the fact that under no circumstances would the military action against the Tamils be allowed to succeed."

This was at a time of 'Take Off' stage when India was entertaining hope of becoming a regional power. This idea, although not new, presumably had been on the drawing boards of Indian strategists for a long time and the Prime Minister of India had once remarked that India would not standby idling if Jaffna was attacked.

It was difficult for me, in military uniform, to take on the Indian High Commissioner due to diplomatic implications. However, on a couple of occasions, I told him very sternly not to hoodwink Sri Lanka any further. Dixit was a crafty man and knew how to slip away when cornered. Although it was against the norms of high military office in Sri Lanka, I clashed with the High Commissioner on many occasions and he knew very well my feelings towards him and India over this intrusion.

The High Commissioner, I knew, was acting firmly on instructions from his superiors. The attitude, the plans, and interpretations made by J.N. Dixit, during that troubled times, were published in his book *Assignment Colombo*, which came out in 1988. In it Dixit says, "I told Lalith (Sri Lanka Minister of Internal Security) when he went on claiming his impending victory, that India would not allow the capture of Jaffna and the persecution of the civilian population there. I told him that if Indian advice was not accepted, India would provide logistical support to the LTTE." Dixit and many other Indian politicians should have understood that there is no solution ever to be gained by encouraging terrorism. This was amply displayed when the LTTE decided to bite the arm that fed them by assassinating Indian Prime Minister Mr. Rajiv Gandhi.

Our forces were professional. We did not make crass decisions. We were skilled and proficient with an uncompromising interest in our country, but there was this man Dixit poking his finger into everything! The Sri Lankan Foreign Minister and her officials had gone to sleep – perhaps they gave into the bullying attitudes of India.

There was one occasion when Dixit was at a loss for words. Dixit who kept on denying that India was training Tamil terrorists got the shock of his life when Ravi Jayawerdene produced a grenade and asked Dixit to have a close look at it. President Jayawardene who was present was startled but was equally shocked to find the words made in India boldly inscribed on the grenade. Ravi had taken care to get the powder removed from the grenade which had been found among a group of LTTE cadres.

After the food dropping gimmick, there was more to come. All military operations were stopped till the politicians settled the issue at large. Discussions behind closed doors were already underway. It was not my business. I did not know what was going on.

The 1987 Peace Accord was finally rammed down President Jayewardene's throat though there was the outward stance of 'agreement.' To his credit, I must say that he never liked it, but had no option. We in the military vehemently disagreed as we were on the verge of crushing terrorism for good.

The suspension of Operation Liberation and signing of the Peace Accord not only demoralized the troops, but all participants in various forms, civilians and the general public who were watching every move with fear and pride. Tensions were running high amongst the population. The Indian Peace Accord was viewed with scepticism by the general public and this became an ideal opportunity for the southern insurgency led by the JVP to take to the streets by protesting the Indian involvement and Peace Accord, which resulted in anti-government riots.

The Peace Accord was a double-edged sword in itself. The outward motives may have been political, but the people protested with vehemence mainly because it was done in a hurry even without the knowledge of some government ministers. President Jayewardene had very little choice in the matter, but succumbed to the pressure as he may have understood the adverse repercussions if he went against India at that juncture. As more details of the Indo-Lanka Peace Accord surfaced in the newspapers, the impending arrival of the Indian Army resulted in the public getting on to the streets in protest. This soon became unruly with the terror that was unleashed in Colombo. Buses and many vehicles were set on fire and there was a complete collapse of law and order. Mayhem had been unleashed in anticipation of the arrival of the Indian Army in Sri Lanka. The protests and destruction of property was quickly spreading towards the deep south where extreme Sinhalese elements made capital out of the situation.

Incidentally the visit of Rajiv Gandhi to Sri Lanka in July 1987 was a nightmare in many ways. It was foresight which prevented a tragedy where a naval rating tried to hit him with the gun. Army and Navy, on the instructions of Ravi Jayewardene the President's son, took care to remove the firing pins and mechanisms of the guns carried by those in the guard of honour as well as the gun powder from the shells that were given out for those in the guard of honour. Some were aghast and said that the armed forces will feel demoralised. If that had been done in Egypt President Sadat would have lived much longer. It was also Ravi who asked President Jayewardene not to accompany Rajiv Gandhi to the guard of honour. Some even say that Rajiv Gandhi was not the target.

The Indo-Lanka Accord was signed on the 29th July 1987. One salient point of the Accord was that all militant groups should surrender their arms within 72 hours of the cessation of hostilities. Finally, India had her way – the Indian Peace Keeping Force (IPKF) arrived in the island on the 30th of July 1987. The 54th Infantry Division of the Indian Army was the first contingent to arrive in the island. I suddenly found myself performing a different role. I felt that although the fighting days with the LTTE was temporarily over, I had to ensure that the Indian forces only carried out what was stipulated in the Accord, and we in the military would not give the IPKF one ounce more of authority in the Peninsula. I was constantly in touch with my Indian counterpart Gen. K. Sunderjee, who was in every sense an officer and a gentleman.

However, I knew he had to carry out Indian Government orders, but was very co-operative. I was also contacted by Southern Indian Army Commander Lt. Gen. Depinder Singh. Those two Indian officers were professionals par excellence.

The arrival of the IPKF meant that some of our troops could be sent to the south to tackle the JVP. The latter led violent demonstrations attacking the arrival of the IPKF, the signing of the Indo Lanka accord and the presence of the IPKF. President Jayewardene permitted Indian helicopters to ferry the troops from Jaffna to the South. I said that they should not use Indian planes to bring back some of the soldiers and instead planes could be used to land in Katunayake and not in Colombo. By then the Ratmalana airport saw high activity as they were using it for civilian flights. I did not want to have a situation where press photographers will see the troop movements and their return from Jaffna by using Indian Planes.

I was informed that Major Gen. Harkirat Singh will command the Indian troops in Sri Lanka. Initially, the old terminal building at the Palaly Airport was handed over to the IPKF to set up base. There was high activity with streams of Indian troops being inducted by air to Palaly and by sea to Kankesanthurai (KKS). Separate groups of IPKF soldiers arrived in Trincomalee as well. On the arrival of those troops in the Northern and Eastern Provinces, the IPKF occupied positions alongside the Sri Lankan forces. Many IPKF soldiers were housed in

Indian makeshift tents. Brig. Gerry De Silva of the Sri Lanka Army who was the Commander of the Security Forces in Jaffna coordinated the induction of IPKF troops with his Indian counterparts.

Harkirat Singh went to Jaffna by jeep soon after the Indian forces landed. He was happy that many who came to welcome the IPKF on the streets of Jaffna were even keen to squat on top of his jeep. Little did he realise that as he allowed them to sit on the jeep *complacency* has already set in and the battle with the LTTE was lost on the top of the jeep bonnet.

I was surprised that though the Indian Army was very disciplined, Major Gen. A.S. Kalkat always came late for meetings. One of the accusations of Dixit was that the IPKF was totally unprepared for the tasks.

We also found a gradual change in Indian attitude when Mr. Prabhakharan suddenly became Prabhakaran, and a few weeks later was downgraded to just Prabakharan, and then finally ended up as 'that bugger'.

In spite of the hue and cry, amidst various negative opinions being aired, I had my own impressions of the IPKF. Without any prejudice, they were a confident lot and the Commander of the IPKF, Major Gen. Harkirat Singh considered it his mission to force the LTTE to hand over arms as promised. If not, he stated, quite nonchalantly that he would 'finish' the LTTE in three weeks.

As much as Prime Minister Rajiv Gandhi gave the Sri Lankan Government various assurances, he in fact gave Prabhakaran his commitment to safe-guard the interests of the LTTE as well. It was obvious that the Peace Accord would serve the central government of India three purposes:

Securing the Tamil Nadu vote base

Asserting authority as a regional partner with a control over the island

Blocking the Trincomalee tank farm and the natural harbour being used by the USA coupled with the setting up of 'Voice of America' relay stations.

Sri Lankan authorities would have considered having a US involvement in the island, like India was doing, getting too involved in the conflict. But India did not want that. Pakistan too was supporting the Sri Lankan Government militarily and it was international politics throttling our island nation.

It was time for the handing over of weapons by the rebels according to the peace agreement. IPKF which was now in northern and eastern parts of Sri Lanka was to overlook and ensure that all weapons were handed over. A few Sri Lankan officials including Secretary Defence, Gen. Sepala Attygalle attended the ceremony. I chose to avoid this and remained at Palaly. The first report reaching us of the weapons handover was that the most ineffective weapons which the LTTE received from the Tamil Nadu government was being handed over. In the military headquarters in Palaly, we conferred and were watching the situation very closely. It was a foregone conclusion that the LTTE's past record of only killing, terrorizing the people and guerrilla methods would satisfy them, and not an honourable peace solution acceptable to all within Sri Lanka. India had to learn the truth the hard way.

However, the surrender of arms and ammunition was being dragged on as either party (IPKF or LTTE) was not sure of what was happening behind the scenes. I raised this issue with Lt. Gen. Depinder Singh, who promptly assured me that all measures were being taken to disarm the Tigers. We were also aware that the LTTE, whilst surrendering the obsolete arms, were shopping for more sophisticated weaponry in the international market. The Indian High Commissioner and Gen. Sunderjee were informed of this dangerous development. Mr. Dixit in his usual exuberant manner dismissed the claim without going into details and these weapons were used against the IPKF by the LTTE subsequently.

At this point, our intelligence picked up vital information that RAW, the intelligence wing of the Indian armed forces, was again up to scuttling the whole peace process by supplying arms to all smaller separatist groups other than the LTTE. I am sure that this had the blessing of those in the higher echelons of the Indian Government and that was the time I raised the issue of Indians having an ulterior motive in the whole exercise at a Security Council meeting attended by Lalith Athulathmudali and Prime Minister Ranasinghe Premadasa.

The Prime Minister could not hide his anger at the revelation and instantly blurted out anti-Indian sentiments and wound up the meeting by assuring that if and when he was the President of the country his first task would be to get rid of the Indians. By this time, Indian High Commissioner J.N. Dixit was known to be giving direct orders to the IPKF bypassing the accepted military chain of command. We discussed these issues at length at regular Security Council meetings and had in place contingency plans for any eventuality. Dixit getting involved in military affairs was the beginning of the end of the honeymoon between the IPKF, and the LTTE. I had credible information that India had different plans in playing a double game with the LTTE. Indians were good at this specially with J.N. Dixit as Indian High Commissioner. It was a matter of time that the Peace Accord broke down and fighting erupted again.

An incident related about Rajiv Gandhi ordering the assassination of Prabhakaran has never been fully investigated. In the book *Intervention in Sri Lanka* by Harkirat Singh (published by Vijitha Yapa Publications, p. 57) he says, 'On the night of 14/15 September 1987, I received a telephone call from Dixit, directing me to arrest or shoot Pirabakaran when he came for the meeting. Telling Dixit that I would get back to him, I placed a call to the Lt. Gen. Depinder Singh directed me to tell Dixit that we, as an orthodox Army, did not shoot people in the back when they were coming for a meeting under the white flag. I then spoke to Dixit in Colombo and conveyed the message emphasising that I would not obey his directive. I pointed out that the LTTE supremo had been invited by the IPKF in order to find a solution to the problems in the implementation of the Accord. Dixit replied, 'He [Rajiv Gandhi] has given these instructions to me and the Army should not drag its feet, and you as the GOC, IPKF will be responsible for it.'

Harkirat Singh says he flew to Jaffna, met Prabakharan and brought him to Palaly by helicopter and Dixit also came for the meeting. After talks, the LTTE delegation preferred to travel by road escorted by their cadres. Harkirat Singh says, 'It was probably this incident that led Dixit to reportedly write to the Government of India on 19th September 1987 that the IPKF was totally unprepared for the task at hand. He also alleged that IPKF commanders were showing extraordinary deference to Pirabakaran, 'even saluting him' and finally he stated that a disastrous situation might develop if GOC 54 Division was not changed.'

That time, if war broke out, we were sure that the Indians would find out whether the early training they gave the guerrillas was effective. After all, it was of their own seeking! The IPKF and Dixit's inability to ensure implementation of various provisions of the Accord led to anti-IPKF feelings. The LTTE saw opportunity there and organized protest marches shouting anti-Indian slogans in the northern theatre. According to the Accord - Sri Lankan troops remained confined to the barracks. These anti-IPKF demonstrations were followed by the LTTE killing a few IPKF soldiers. Gen. Sunderjee flew to Sri Lanka and had extensive discussions with me about the latest developments. He was testing the water for a ground offensive by the IPKF against the LTTE. It was evident that the Indian Army was going to induct more fighting brigades to the north and east of Sri Lanka. The IPKF was just about to start from where we were forced to stop – Operation Liberation.

General Sundarjee, the Indian Army Commander, was an honourable officer and would not do any nonsense. Once when I came back to my office I was surprised to see an Indian officer waiting for me. It is only when I came close to him that I realised that this was the Indian Commander, General Sundarjee. I was shocked, I asked him "I thought you will be with High Commissioner Dixit". He said,

122

"I don't want to see Dixit or big shit. I want to see you. Tell me what is happening." He did not care for politicians or diplomats; he was a professional soldier.

I remember once visiting his headquarters in Delhi, Dixit was there as well as an Indian Minister Mr. Pant. Dixit started a long harangue about various things in Sri Lanka. I listened to him patiently and told him, "You don't have to come to Delhi to tell me all this; you should have told me in Colombo. If you had a problem you should have told me." Sundarjee realised I was angry and said, 'Please don't get angry; there are diplomats and there are politicians.' I said, "I say what I have to say."

In a twist of fate, the Sri Lankan Navy arrested 17 LTTE cadres trying to cross over from India with a cache of arms. As this was in the territorial waters of Sri Lanka, the navy had the authority to take any person carrying arms into custody. The IPKF desperately tried to get involved to seek the release of the arrested cadres, but we had to apply the law of the land immaterial of caste, creed or religion. This was one instance where IPKF tried to step out of the boundaries demarcated in the Peace Accord.

A firm decision was made to shift the arrested LTTE cadres to Colombo and the law to be applied to them as to any other Sri Lankans. Lalith Athulathmudali insisted they should be brought to stand trial to Colombo. To him a bird in the hand was better that two in the bush. Whether the Cyanide capsules were smuggled to them or whether they already had it with them, when they were captured is unknown. But that decision went to the LTTE. I told the IPKF I can't release them as it is a political decision taken in Colombo. 'My decision is final and please make your representations to Colombo..'

The LTTE hierarchy never knew the word "law of the land" and pressurized the Sri Lankan Government through the IPKF for the release. When the arrested cadres knew that all efforts for their release was futile, they took cyanide and committed suicide. The LTTE leadership put the blame squarely on the IPKF for not being able to secure the release, which further soured the relationship between the two parties. With neither party wanting openly to declare war, sporadic clashes took place in both Northern and Eastern Provinces between the IPKF and the LTTE. It was a matter of time before a full-scale war broke out. The LTTE was to face the fourth largest army in the world on their home terrain. More sophisticated weapons, heavy artillery and fighting brigades were inducted while the LTTE too were getting ready for another guerrilla battle.

It was sad to hear of the killing of the Ven. Rambukkana Saddhalankara Thera in Trincomalee. I went to Trincomalee and asked the IPKF 'Why don't you do something about this' 'The IPKF officer replied what I can under the circumstances.' On another occasion I was asked to wait while they made arrangements to provide transport for me to visit one of the remote villages where there had been a violent attack by the LTTE. I told the IPKF, 'You are the IPKF but if you are can't control their situation we will have to take action'. They would not allow me to go to the village and I told them, 'I do not accept your restriction on my movements. This is my country and I go where 'I want. I told him the LTTE is on the run but they are running the place.'

The IPKF underestimated the LTTE. The Indians thought that they knew everything. Therefore they did not want any help from the Sri Lanka army. They didn't want to listen to our views or consult us on our ground knowledge and intelligence.

When the first armoured tanks of the Indians were used in the north some machines got bogged down because they did not know the ground realties. They had no modern maps of Sri Lanka. Thus on a number of occasions the LTTE changed the name boards of the roads and the Indian Army ended up going in the wrong direction.

The Indian Army consisted of over a million troops and was more modernized than ours, with combat experience in fighting terrorism in their own country in similar conditions. Secondly, the Indian Navy was well equipped with a long reach supported by electronic devices to combat LTTE transmissions. The Indian Air Force was similarly equipped to enable easy air mobility and they possessed equipment including armoured fighting vehicles supported by helicopters and gun ships.

Thirdly, the IPKF had adequate personnel who spoke the Tamil language while at the same time possessing cultural affinities to the LTTE and the Tamil population in the Jaffna Peninsula. Many operations and offensives by the IPKF were launched to tame the Tigers. By March 1990, nearly two and a half years had lapsed since the arrival of the IPKF. Their task was still incomplete with a growing amount of casualties and debts, which I guess at that point was demoralizing for the IPKF.

India may have thought that Sri Lanka would be a piece of cake, just like Bangaladesh. The Indians trained the Mukti Bahini on Indian soil and when the correct time came let them loose. They began to fight the Pakistanis but at the same time were of great assistance when the Indians decided to enter East Pakistan (later Bangladesh). It is these Mukthi Bahini who encouraged the Bangladeshis to welcome the Indians with open arms. It is this same type of reception that Indians expected in northern Sri Lanka from the LTTE and others whom they had trained and armed. But they did not reckon with the ruthlessness of the LTTE and their long term plans. The Indians thought that when they said move, everyone will jump. By the time they discovered that it did not quite work that way, the tide had turned, and no longer were the Indians looked on as saviours by the ordinary people.

While India was able to control the Bangladeshis, the issue was different with regard to Sikkim where after the Chogyals were dismissed from power the territory was absorbed into India. The story of Kashmir is in some ways another tragic event in Indian history, and is still smouldering

The IPKF lost over 1,000 fighting soldiers in the battle against the LTTE but continued to hold ground. Amidst all the happenings in the north and east between IPKF and LTTE, the Presidential elections in Sri Lanka took place and another era was to begin…

President Jayewardene said he intends to promote me to the rank of Field Marshall which I opposed vehemently. He said that the Minister of National Security and Deputy Minister of Defence Lalith Athulathmudali was also in agreement with him. But I said that I do not deserve a promotion to Field Marshall as this honour is given to military leaders who have been involved in major wars against another nation.

President Premadasa

With the election of Premadasa as President and the dawn of a new era, one significant change took place – the retreat of the IPKF. This total pull-out marked the fulfilment of one of the main pledges given by President Premadasa at the 1988 December Presidential election campaign. Two and a half years after the signing of the Indo-Lanka accord on 29th July 1987, the IPKF left Sri Lanka's shores from the Petroleum Jetty in China Bay on board the Indian Naval ship 'Magar,' meaning crocodile in Hindi!

On my part, I believed that the ordering of the immediate withdrawal of the IPKF by the newly elected President was a mistake. The IPKF, had they remained, would somehow have managed to complete their mission of destroying the LTTE terrorism: the very terrorists they themselves had trained not too long ago. With their departure, the Sri Lankan forces took over.

With the fallen numbers and heavy military action, the LTTE had considerably weakened. A consequence of this was that they strived to make contact with newly appointed President Premadasa, knowing all too well that he was receptive to discussion.

The President on his part misjudged the LTTE. The LTTE had a game plan of its own. On the pretext of finding a peaceful solution, the LTTE pressurized the government into starting negotiations. The strategy they used was to employ front organizations worldwide. This gave them enough time which they used for their advantage. As the fruitless negotiations progressed, the LTTE used the halt of an offensive to strengthen their cadre, collect finances, train their cadre, re-equip their artillery while at the same time, maintaining a clear interest in the Tamil diaspora to prove to the international community, their interest and participation in the democratic process of negotiations.

Soon after being elected, President R. Premadasa invited me for a discussion, which took place at his office in Flower Road. What followed was least unexpected. He requested me to be his Secretary of Defence. I thanked him and declined the offer as I had done so when the previous President J.R. Jayewardene requested me to be his Secretary of Defence. The President at that time was indeed kind enough to accommodate my views, but he requested me to be his advisor on matters pertaining to Defence. This, I had to accept.

At the same time, I was also holding the substantive appointment of the Chairman, Airport and Aviation Services (SL) Ltd. It was indeed with surprise that I opened the Daily News one particular morning which had my photograph on the front page, stating that I was appointed Secretary to the Minister of State for Defence while, Mr. Ranjan Wijeratne will be additional Secretary of Defence.

I was indeed not enamoured by the press notice, to say the least. Subsequently, I met Mr. Wijeratne, who was a Colonel in the SLRC (Sri Lanka Rifle Corps), who served during the LTTE insurrection under JOC. It was then that I informed him that the press notice was unacceptable, as I had refused the offer; not once, but twice – once under former President J.R. Jayewardene. However, my conscience served the better of me at that point. I admit that I felt that it was discomforting to walk out at this point and let down my country in such a manner. Reluctantly, I agreed to hold this post for a short period of time until another suitable person could be recruited for the post, whom I promised to train personally.

In an official capacity, the Secretary of Defence had to ensure proper financial discipline in the services and police while maintaining expenses within estimates as provided for in the budget, and where necessary, prepare supplementary estimates for approval of the government. I was at that time fortunate to have the services of very good accountants in Mr. Gunawardane and Brig. Granville Elapatha who were honourable as well as extremely reliable.

Procurement of equipment through tender procedures was made tremendously easy for me as the chief accounting officer of the Ministry of Defence. The procurement committee we started at JOC continued with Mr. Nimal Jayawardane, a much respected economist cum lawyer as its Chairman.

R. Premadasa was a person who was totally committed to developing Sri Lanka. He was very keen to go into the villages at Gam Udawa and insisted on displaying the latest Army equipment. My men had to camp out for weeks and explain to the thousands who thronged the grounds how the various weapons worked. Once I asked him what is the purpose of taking these armoured cars and equipments to remote villages? Immediately he retorted. "So you are also one of those who want to have exhibitions in Colombo 7, where people come, gossip and go away. Through Gam Udawa I am taking them to the villages, the remote areas of this land. They know a lot about of this country and what our country is. Most of them will see it for the first time." I saw the purpose of his vision when I realised that looking back it is these villages which provided the boys for the army.

Ranjan Wijeratne was in charge of security but unfortunately he had precise movements which meant that everyone knew what his movements in the morning were. At 8.30 a.m. each morning he would venture out. He always took the same route along Havelock Road to go to his office. When I told him that his security was very poor, he pulled out from his purse a scrap of paper and gave it to me and said, "This give details of the Rahu Kalaya." I told him I did not believe it. He thanked me for my concern and continued' and the result was an unnecessary death. My first reaction on hearing of the deadly bomb was one of anger. I was also security conscious but I never went on the same road. I often walked in my shorts and no one knew who I was. All those who were blown up on the roads were those who went around in posh cars and jeeps, very often with escorts.

The most shocking incident in my career was when I discovered by accident that President Premadasa had decided to give arms to the

LTTE. Brigadier Bhoran was waiting to see General Atygalle, and when I asked him what he wanted, he replied "I came to take the weapons", I asked him, "What weapons?" He said, "The weapons we are giving to the LTTE." I was in a state of shock. It was the first I had heard about it but I had to pretend that I knew about it. I said, "Ok you better meet General Attygalle, "and went to the adjoining office. I later marched into General Atygalle's office and said, "I can't believe this. Brigadier Bhoran says he has come to take weapons to the LTTE. What are these weapons and who ordered them. This is madness. Sheer Madness."

General Atygalle said, "You better ask the President; this is his idea." I used the General's hotline and spoke to President Premadasa. It was about 5.00 p.m. in the evening. He said, "I have very busy programs and can't see you now. Can you see me at 5.00 a.m. tomorrow morning at Sucharitha?"

Next morning when I saw him, President Premadasa was in shorts doing exercises. He wanted to know what I wanted. I said, "Sir, it was last evening I heard you are sending weapons to the LTTE."

'Why? asked. I replied, "How can you give weapons to the LTTE? What about the IPKF who are engaged in wiping out the LTTE? What about India?"

President Premadasa replied, "I will sort it out. They have assured me they will never fight us with these weapons. I am giving them these arms to fight the TNA (Tamil National Army) which the IPKF is creating. "He must have seen my anger because he showed me a copy of *India Today* and asked, "Have you read this?" The article contained information about the Tamil National Army.

'You are giving weapons to terrorists. My life has been spent fighting with them. Please stop it. They are going through Padaviya to deliver it, an area where many Sinhala villagers had been killed by the LTTE." Premadasa was annoyed and said, "I can't change it now." I told him, "It is my duty to tell you; it is your prerogative to make a decision." He was vivid with anger.

I was crying as I left. Should I send in my resignation? I told Myrtle that I am fed up and I am not going to office. I don't want anyone to think I was a party to giving arms to the LTTE.

Myrtle tried to pacify me and I barked at her and said, "I don't need advise from you." There was silence.

As much as I enjoyed the nature of my work, I had to face immense inner turmoil. I had to stand by at that time and watch certain incidents taking place without being able to do anything about it as I was not vested with such authority. To this day, I will maintain, that I did voice my opinion. I voiced my protest and had to stand by and watch the LTTE being provided with arms. I was horrified. I had no say against the hierarchy.

It was at that point that I realized the futility of it all. All that I had done for my country suddenly became of no use. The principles I had always maintained right from the very start when I led the campaigns against the LTTE, were being compromised not by me but by other individuals whose voices were stronger than mine.

The LTTE was provided with arms for reasons anyone could still inquire into. It was at this point in time that the government was faced with the trouble that was being caused by the TNA (Tamil National Army). The TNA incidentally was a proxy army that was created by the IPKF and India to maintain law and order in the northeast after the departure of the Indian Army. President Premadasa had always been suspicious of the Indian designs vis-à-vis Sri Lanka. He had after all neutralized the JVP rhetoric against Indian 'imperialism' by unilaterally making certain that the Indian troops withdrew from Sri Lanka. The TNA he despised, as he believed that there was no room in the country for two armies.

The TNA had questionable origins. I recall General Kalkat once having the cheek to ask me to provide the TNA with arms. I staunchly refused. I refused not only to give even a single weapon, but even to participate in such a discussion.

The LTTE used the weapons they obtained from our government to fight the TNA. At the same time, using the ceasefire that was a vital part of the negotiations that had just gotten underway between them and the Sri Lankan Government, to strengthen their forces and make up for their loss. After a brief three-month interlude of peace, the LTTE broke the ceasefire agreement and recommenced their campaign with vigour.

The outcome of everything that was taking place pushed me into a state of despair. I wanted to resign. But I didn't. What stopped me from handing in my resignation as the Secretary Defence, on those fateful days, was the sole thought that the country needed me. I was surrounded with death and destruction: large-scale buildings were being burnt, people were dying.

I could not pack my bags and retire to the safe space of my home. I was needed, I felt. Thus, I remained.

Defamation 1

I was always conscious of the fact that leading a public life has its positive associations, and maybe to a larger extent, drastic negative implications as well. My life in the military has always made me somewhat of a public figure, whether I liked it or not. My feelings were never of any consequence. Every action I took whilst in the military, even as GOC of the JOC and finally as Secretary Defence, were applauded by many, and at the same time criticized and questioned by more. The simplest strategy was to smile with the applause and deal with the punches, I always thought! Needless to say, this approach always worked.

7th July 1992, brought about a different turn of events. I was still Secretary Defence. The *Observer* Editorial published a Comment titled, "Who is attacking the army now?" While implicitly praising Lt. Gen. Cecil Waidyaratne, Admiral Clancy Fernando and Air Marshal Terence Gunawardane for their conducting of smooth and successful operations in the north and praising their leadership which was 'supposed' to be steering the campaign to win peace in the north, my position as the former GOC was harshly criticized:

"The achievements of the three Service Commanders – Lt. Gen. Cecil Waidyaratne, Admiral Clancy Fernando and Air Marshal Terence Gunawardane – are remarkable. The strategic operations, coordinated with the fullest cooperation of the three commanders, are moving smoothly in the north. The total gains so far speak eloquently for the hard work, clear thinking and the calibre of leadership that is now steering the campaign to win peace in the north....

"The gains of the forces in driving the terrorists away from their entrenched positions have boosted the morale, the image and the determination of the army, which is inching its way forward. Under

Lt. Gen. Waidyaratne the forces have scored success after success. This is in stark contrast to the disasters under the JOC operations which were headed by Gen. Hamilton Wanasignhe and Gen. Cyril Ranatunga. The army hit rock bottom with key camps in Kattiparichchan, Kokavil and Mankulam falling ignominiously into the hands of the Tigers. The Tigers ran over these camps with great ease. On those occasions, Gen. Ranatunga would hastily summon a press conference to give excuses. Those were embarrassing moments for the army and the nation. Today under Lt. Gen. Waidyaratne the army does not give excuses. It advances slowly, but surely.

7th July 1992 *Observer*

The *Observer* Editorial from which I have quoted above was written by H.L.D. Mahindapala, the Editor of the *Observer*. Not only had he slandered my reputation as a retired military man – a person who had done immense service to his country – but he had also cast the army and the JOC in an unfavourable light. The manner in which he wielded the pen, was unforgivable.

The reason behind all this controversy was a deeper conflict of interest. The article had been instigated by Lt. Gen. Waidyaratne, who I had thought unsuitable for the post of the Chief of Staff to take command of the army after Gen. Hamilton Wanasinghe. My personal recommendation was Brig. Denzil Kobbekaduwa. Since I never believed in doing anything behind any individual's back, I in my capacity as Defence Secretary summoned Lt. Gen. Waidyaratne to my office, He thought I was going to recommend him as Army Commander. I said I had made my decision and he should be the first to know, showed him my recommendation and pointed out to him why I thought that he was unsuitable for the post. He was aghast and went berserk. His many protests did leave me feeling rather perturbed and made me question my decision, but this was not a personal matter – I was choosing someone on behalf of the army and on behalf of Sri Lanka, my country. My feelings were insignificant. This was the start of the campaign against me. Soon afterwards, my actions started to be questioned in the papers such as in the Comment, *Observer*:

The JOC, which is now headed by Gen. Wanasinghe should keep their unwanted fingers out of the operations that are hitting their targets accurately. From the days of the disastrous Vadamaarachchi campaign both Gen. Wanasinghe and Gen. Ranatunga have failed to score significant victories.

Beginning from the Vadamaarachchi campaign the army treated campaigns more as a teledrama to portray them as medal-winning heroes, covering up, of course, their failure to roll back the tide of Tiger terrorists.

Within a short period of six months Lt. Gen. Waidyaratne had injected a new moral code, enforced discipline which was lacking earlier, introduced special training courses for officers fighting in the frontline, checked corruption and wasteful practices, and, above all, elevated the army to a professional level.

7th July 1992, *Observer*

The article left me questioning my own standing. What I realized subsequently was that if I started questioning my standing, what would the people of this nation believe? The power of the pen, I always believed, was mightier than the sword. Therefore, not content to sit aside and let others have the final say, I decided to file action against Mr. Mahindapala for defamation. With the initial paperwork being drawn up by the lawyers from the law firm Perera and Abeysekara, I prepared to sue the *Observer* for publishing false and detrimental material against me.

However, the case never got underway. I was personally summoned by President Premadasa to the Presidential Secretariat where I was asked to come into a room; and there was Mr. Mahindapala standing meekly alongside the President. He was asked to apologize to me, which he did.

But I realized at that moment, that an apology received in the closed vicinity of the Presidential Secretariat would not appease me. I refused the apology and informed the President that I would only accept an apology, if it should appear in the papers itself. The Editor meekly agreed and left the premises as hastily as he could.

The unwanted publicity given by Gen. Waidyaratne through people like Mr. Mahindapala, the Editor of the *Observer* not only brought disrepute to the Armed Forces but was a complete demoralizer. Such actions only became another feather in the cap of the terrorists... Unfortunately, no action was taken against the Lake House group, Mr. Mahindapala, the Editor of the *Observer*, or Gen. Waidyaratne. The criticism of Gen. Wanasinghe and me as provoked by Gen. Waidyaratne was absolutely anti-nationalistic.

Consequently, an apology did appear in the papers. The apology read:

The Board of Directors of the Associated Newspapers of Ceylon Ltd and the Editor of the *Ceylon Observer* regret the false and malicious references to General Cyril Ranatunga contained in the *Ceylon Observer* of 7th July 1992 in the editorial comment entitled "Who is attacking the Army now?" The said article has been written by Mr. H.L.D. Mahindapala who was then functioning as the Editor of the *Ceylon Observer*. The charges in the said article against General Ranatunga are totally untrue and are hereby withdrawn and any pain of mind and damage caused to General Ranatunga's reputation are regretted.

In hindsight, I now realize that my initial recommendation of Brig. Denzil Kobbekaduwa taking command instead of Gen. Waidyaratne, had it followed through, would have brought about immense changes. Instead, the appointment made, has done nothing but cost the army and the nation very dearly.

In stark contrast to what was said in "Who is attacking the army now?" another Editorial in the *Sun* dated 29th June 1989 was in a completely different light. Titled 'Discipline in the Forces,' the article went on to mention that:

> General Cyril Ranatunga a soldier par excellence has reportedly given out some resourceful advice to the military and police cadres now engaged in restoring law and order in the country.
>
> He had underlined the foremost need of the militia and the police to conduct themselves with a high level of restraint as the assignment before them is very delicate and vulnerable, as it is crucial for the survival of this country as a sovereign and democratic state.
>
> Gen. Ranatunga, the former military supremo now holding the coveted post of Secretary Defence is well versed and experienced in the field of law enforcement and in the difficult task to maintaining discipline among a set of raw recruits who have been taken in en masse to meet a national exigency.

Exemplary

> His record has been exemplary and he is a very respected soldier in the country today.
>
> His appeal to the security forces has come at a time when they are being increasingly assigned to non-combat tasks like the maintenance of law and order.
>
> The wide and sweeping powers that have been bestowed upon the military and police under the state of emergency could sometimes be misused or misinterpreted by the rank and file, thus causing serious political complications or give rise to queries relating to fundamental rights. The General's laudable advice to his men evidently stems from the need to avoid these pitfalls.
>
> To quote his own admirable words, "We should conduct ourselves as highly disciplined men who have been given the great

responsibility of restoring law and order. We should be an example to our fellow citizens..."

The General must have had good reasons too in making this entreaty. In the not too distant past soldiers and policemen have come under public rebuke and even international reprimand for some of their acts of omission and commission. In fact some of them were castigated for the lack of discipline. Even today this predicament has not been really overcome.

Confidence

But the fact that the top brass is making an earnest effort to clean up the image and make the armed forces a truly disciplined lot is most praiseworthy. General Ranatunga deserves the gratitude of the people and the right recognition by the political leadership.

Polishing up the image of the military and that of the police is not an easy task. It is a very cumbersome process.

It needs the psychological and administrative orientation. It must also be a joint effort and done on the basis of strict non-partisanship. Those who fail and falter in their bounden duty and discipline must face the consequences without fear or favour.

The services would have achieved a certain degree of high disciplinary standard when the citizenry could look up to them with a certain respect and confidence. The General knows it. And is admittedly determined to ensure the fait accompli.

29th June 1989, *Sun*

This Editorial served to lighten my heavy heart and gave a sense of faith and hope which had been shattered with the publication of the earlier Editorial. The readers should please note the animosity generated by interested individuals or parties for their selfish gains at the expense of the country by supporting insurgents/terrorists. If very serious servicemen like the army commander could sponsor and support such

138

allegations one could imagine the effect on the morale of the nation in general and security force personnel in particular.

No wonder the war drags on!

My position as the Secretary Defence came to a close when one morning, I received a call from President Premadasa who informed me that Mr. E.L.B. Hurulle had returned from Australia, having completed his term as the Sri Lankan High Commissioner to Australia. He requested me to take his place as the next High Commissioner, to which I promptly agreed. It was only on my way to Australia that I heard the tragic news of the assassination of President Premadasa by a suicide bomber on the streets of Colombo at the May Day procession in 1993. The suicide attack was to have been carried out by a LTTE member who had slowly succeeded in gaining the confidence of the President to the extent of having worked in his private office, Sucharita. Apart from the demise of the President being a complete stab in the back on the part of the LTTE, I was dismayed. The country had once again lost a leader and descended into a state of chaos...

Australia

Prior to my departure to Australia, I met the High Commissioner for Australia in Sri Lanka, Mr. Howard Debbenum. It was he who advised me on how to adjust to this new life altogether and briefed us on diplomatic life in Canberra. My arrival in Australia on 1st May 1993 marked a digression from a life of military preoccupation and heralded a newer walk of life.

On arrival in Canberra, I called on the Foreign Minister Mr. Gareth Evans who was extremely cordial and extended a warm welcome. I presented my credentials to the Governor General which was received with a favourable response from the Australian media. It was shortly afterwards that a Tamil expatriate, Prof. Eliezer, appeared on Australian national television stating rather vehemently that I ought to not be accepted by the Australian Government. According to him, I was responsible for the genocide in Jaffna. I was crushed momentarily but my faith was immediately restored as the very next day, Mr. Gareth Evans issued a statement to the Australian media maintaining that the Government of Australia was pleased and felt privileged to have me as the Sri Lankan High Commissioner; which silenced the Tamil lobby effectively. In the meantime, in Sri Lanka, following the assassination of President Premadasa, Mr. D.B. Wijetunga assumed office as the President of Sri Lanka.

Meanwhile, I was settling in magnificently... Seeing the state of the office of the Sri Lanka High Commission, I managed to obtain four acres of land in the diplomatic enclave, which would enable me to start immediate construction of a new office for the High Commission alongside the quarters for the staff. The money for this was raised by the sale of the former premises to the Australian Government, which was anxious to buy the land and premises occupied by us in order to make way for a much larger plan which involved the redevelopment of Canberra. What I figured was that with the sale of that building, we could construct what will be our new office and save a certain percentage of it as well.

Not being one to delay the implementation of any plan, I called Mr. Wickrema Gunawardane, who was an architect cum engineer who was settled in Melbourne along with his family. He was constructing houses under the name of his new organization and was selling them to the public. I invited him to come to Canberra and have a look at our newly acquired land in order to start work on our High Commission complex. He was happy to oblige and agreed readily with me that the present building we were occupying, was highly unsuitable for a diplomatic mission! After staying with us for a few days, he worked out a detailed plan without any cost to the government and immediately I followed up on it by submitting the plans to the Foreign Ministry in Colombo.

I had no response. The waiting period grew even longer. Shortly afterwards I did receive a telephone call. But it was not the one I was expecting. The Foreign Secretary, Mr. Bernard Tillekeratne called me regarding a pressing matter. A subsequent call from President's Secretary, Mr. K.H.J. Wijedasa followed.

I was to leave Australia immediately and proceed to England where I would be the newly appointed High Commissioner to the Court of S. James, London. This was an order issued directly by the newly appointed President. Needless to say, I was indeed astounded. After expressing my initial astonishment, I politely refused this offer asserting that I was just about to start my official work in Canberra. Also, as the High Commissioner of Australia, I was accredited to New Zealand and Papua New Guinea. I had at that point made arrangements to proceed to both places in order to present my credentials to the relevant authorities.

My decision was absolute. I was not going to change my mind, until I received a call from the President himself. This left me with no alternative. I had to leave Australia. I immediately proceeded to cancel my arrangements and made plans to proceed to London via Sri Lanka;

so that I could enjoy a few days at home with my sons and family. But I was ordered not to do so; I was to fly directly to London, which I did. That, to all intents and purposes, ended my brief four-month spell in Australia as the Sri Lankan High Commissioner. It was much later that I found out the reason behind the hurried decision making: The President had wanted to post a close friend of his as the High Commissioner in Australia. However, why it was so urgent I could never understand... all my plans to meet the pressing needs to the Sri Lankan High Commission in Australia could never materialize under my supervision. Instead I had to content myself with forwarding a written brief outlining my intended changes to the incoming High Commissioner.

Defamation 2

During my short stay in Australia, I had to deal with the most unexpected turn of events: events which shocked me, grieved me and distressed me, as my integrity and character had been duly challenged. One fateful day, towards the end of June, 1993 I received many calls from my family and from my friends expressing their concern. The cause of this turmoil and disturbance was the publishing of an article in the *Lakdiva* newspaper on 20 June 1993 titled 'Cyril Ranatunga yuddaya gasa kala.' A photograph of myself was placed right next to the overwhelming headline. Shortly afterwards I received a copy of the newspaper by courier and as I perused and read through the first page and the ensuing stories on pages 8 and 9, I was deeply affronted. My public service career spanning over 43 years, which I carried out with loyalty and dedication, was tarnished by the article. I kept insisting to the people who called me that there was absolutely no truth in any of the allegations which were made against me. I was adamant that everything I did during my service period of 43 years was carried out with good faith, sincerity and dedication. This publication, I believed, caused immense damage to my reputation.

The article on the front page – the lead – made the following allegations against me:

Primarily, that I had taken commission when purchasing ammunition for the armed forces and that I had cancelled tenders and resorted to other means of procurement for the purchase of T56 rifles, hand grenades, tear gas and bombs etc. It was clearly stated that in spite of the presence of many other tenderers, I had given the tender to NORINCO of China. It went on to declare that I was the representative of NORINCO and that the government had purchased all supplies from them, only because I had brought undue pressure upon the government.

The article went on to state that 15,000 T84 and 81 weapons were purchased at $232 when the price was $135; thereby making a profit of $6.5 million.

The article concluded by stating that no one had dared protest since the concerned parties were frightened of President Premadasa.

20ᵗʰ June 1993, *Lakdiva* (My translation)

In my defence, I categorically denied these allegations. As GOC of the JOC and as the Secretary to the Ministry of Defence, I had always adhered to all procedures as laid down by the government. In fact, the Minister of Defence, The President, the State Minister, Mr. Ranjan Wijeratne and the Prime Minister were unanimous in the decision that we should always adhere to the correct procedure. We constantly had a safeguard where the tender board proceedings were put to a special Cabinet Sub-Committee before it was put up to the Cabinet by the Minister of Defence. No purchases were made without a firm recommendation by the Service Commanders or the Inspector General, Police.

The contention that I was the representative of NORINCO, I found most disconcerting. NORINCO was/is a government organization from China, which has been our suppliers for many years, even at a time when I was GOC, JOC (September 1985-July 88) and long before I took over as Secretary, Defence (February 1990-April 93). At a time when all manufacturing countries refused sales and end user licence to Sri Lanka, NORINCO was the only organization that volunteered to help us out in our time of need. Apart from never having cancelled tenders, let alone being an agent for any organization, I still maintain that purchases from NORINCO were always on tender and that purchases without a tender procedure were never adopted. In brief, the whole world and any interested party knew that we dealt with NORINCO on a government-to-government basis and all the statements made in the article (front page) were false, defamatory and above all an insult to the credibility of the entire Defence establishment.

As if one story was not enough to make the point, the Editor of *Lakdiva* had printed a bigger version of the same front page story titled 'Hamuda Bhatayan-Vesiyan Mareddi Mun Dollar Gilala' continuing along the same defamatory line. The centre page article also made unrelenting preposterous accusations:

It compared the war to the narcotics trade – in a manner that the attitude exercised by senior officials in the Defence Ministry was no different to that of drug lords.

Secondly, the article spoke of the purchase of the Pucara aircraft and M18 helicopters, once again implying that I had sought an immense commission through the purchase.

20th June 1993, *Lakdiva (*My translation*)*

Regarding the purchase of the M18 helicopters, the tender board followed every necessary step. The purchase was recommended by the Air Force Commander and his technical officers. It was at that point we were officially informed by the Russian Ambassador that there would be no guarantee in the supply of spare parts if we were to make the purchase from outside sources. The tender board, to my recollection, evaluated the tenders and recommended the purchase which was an unbelievable bargain coming from the manufacturers themselves. It was at that point in time that I was faced with the unfortunate task of fending off agents, suppliers both from Sri Lanka and abroad, who were disappointed with my not wanting to meet them in my official capacity, by directing them to the tender board.

The T85 tanks or armoured vehicles, both wheeled and tracked, were selected based on the recommendations of the army, which had comprised of a special board consisting very senior armoured corps officers who had suggested these to the Army Commander. I had no hand in the evaluation in general. But we were faced with a catch-22 type situation as no country agreed to sell them to us, including China. It was only after the strategic intervention of Mr. Ranjan Wijeratne and myself by approaching the Foreign Minister of China, during the visit of Prime Minister Li Peng to Sri Lanka, that we were able to secure the sale of the T85 armoured vehicles.

The seemingly controversial acquisition of the Pucara aircraft was a completely different story in all, as pointed out in detail before when I spoke of how procurement occurred at the Joint Operations Command. Instead of resorting to repetition, I simply rest my case. The only statement I can make is that to the best of my knowledge, the Pucara is a dedicated anti-terrorist operational aircraft with superior fire power and, payload, and that it possessed a much greater endurance. It also included the additional safety factor of two engines.

The only purchase that was made outside the tender procedure was the purchase of the MBTs – T55 tanks: again this came to us as a proposal from the Army Headquarters a matter of top secrecy. I was not pleased with the confidentiality of the deal and requested our High Commissioner in London to check on the credibility of this offer. The immediate reaction to my request was an urgent missive from the proposing party of this package informing the Ministry, that if we were to give the deal any publicity, it would be duly cancelled. This was the only deal about which we faced many problems, in spite of the necessary precautions being taken from our side; even to the extent of sending a very powerful team of senior army officers to inspect the equipment prior to shipment.

While I am content to state for the record here the falsity of the allegations made by P.G. Rohana Kumara and K.M. Thilak Wehella, the publishers and the Editor of the *Lakdiva* newspaper, I promptly filed action. Daya Perera, a leading counsel advised me to retain the services of Ben Eliatamby, a leading lawyer.

Though the case dragged on over a considerable period of time, on 14th March 1994, the High Court of Colombo deemed that both Rohana Kumara and Thilak Wehella were guilty of defamation and ordered them to tender an unconditional apology to me for the pain of mind and damage caused to my reputation as a result of the false publication. On my part, I refused any money – I did not want to be compensated. Instead, I insisted that they first publish an apology as a news item in the front page of the following papers: The *Sunday Observer, Sunday Lankadeepa, The Sunday Times, Sunday Diwaina, Sunday Island* and *Silumina.* As for compensation, I was adamant that the accused donate a sum of money as ordered by the court to the Weera Sebala Foundation, which they did at a later stage. The apology appeared in all the papers I had mentioned shortly afterwards.

The apology appearing in The Sunday Island read:

"Thilak Wehella, Rohana Kumara Tender Our Apologies to General Cyril Ranatunga

We deeply tender out apologies for the *discremate/* defamatory statements published in the *Lakdiva* Newspaper of 20th June 1993, against defence secretary Cyril Ranatunga, this statement is free from truth.

If this statement has caused any untoward reputation to disgrace your *charactor* we deeply *regrest* and tender our apologies for same.

21st May 1995, *The Island*

The Queen's English it certainly was not! With all due respect, it was republished after the mistakes were rectified. It was only then that I could rest easy...

Court of S. James, London

Getting to England, having to put aside all my commitment in Australia, was without doubt not an easy undertaking. The flight from Canberra to London itself was strenuous and exceptionally tiring. Having reached London, I immediately moved into my official residence at Avenue Road, St. John's Wood. At this stage, I was disappointed – disappointed at not being able to see through my intended plans in Australia, where I had just begun to settle in after having adjusted to a new way of life. But in retrospect, I feel I settled in rather swiftly... I learnt to adjust to what was dealt my way.

Heading my list of duties, I was to present my credentials to Her Majesty the Queen at Buckingham Palace. The ceremony was extremely formal. The Protocol Officers had called on us earlier and briefed us on the procedures. It certainly was different and novel! I rode in a horse carriage while Myrtle followed close behind in my car. We had met the Queen earlier when I was at the Royal College of Defence Studies in 1974, when she visited the College. At this protocol ceremony however, she spoke with us on many matters: one of which was regarding her previous visit to Sri Lanka. It made me proud to hear her speak so well of our country... It was a time when I had started to begin feeling disillusioned about what was happening here, but to hear Her Majesty speak well of my nation, caused an immense upsurge of pride within myself. This meeting with the Queen was not the last of our encounters with her. One such occasion was when we had the privilege of being invited to a garden party at the Buckingham Palace on the event of her birthday. We were amongst a considerable number of other Sri Lankans!

It was during my term in London that I invited General Sir Michael Rose who was the United National Commander of the Forces in Bosnia for dinner. Among the guests was Ranil Wickremasinghe. We subsequently spent a weekend at his home. When Ranil

Wickremasinghe became the Prime Minister in 2002 he rang me and asked whether, General Sir Michael Rose could be invited to visit Sri Lanka. He visited Sri Lanka and went to all the operational areas and spoke to the officers (see annexure 1)

Life in London was not relaxed or tranquil in the least. I was unquestionably busy at all hours, as London was home to a large Sri Lankan community and an equally large number of diplomatic missions. Most evenings, I had not one but a number of gatherings to attend. I still cannot recall how I managed it all; but I think I dealt with it rather successfully.

It was a time when I went from one party or congregation to another, having done nothing but showing my mere presence for a couple of minutes to let it known that I had been there! The Commonwealth Office in London organized a large number of activities, and member countries that took precedence over non-member countries, had to attend such events. Most evenings therefore, as stated before, were occupied attending functions in foreign embassies or in one of the many Sri Lankan organizations.

Whilst gradually getting used to the demanding life the High Commissioner of London was supposed to lead, I noticed a matter which soon became a pressing concern on my part. I realized that there was a considerable amount of reluctance exercised on the part of the majority of the Sri Lankan Tamil community to visit the High Commission except for pressing, urgent matters, such as collecting of passports or the re-issuing of visas. To remedy this, I decided to invite the expatriate Tamil community, through the means of some of my Tamil friends, to the High Commission for tea. I was surprised: I had a very good response! My next step was to extend an invitation to members of both the Sinhalese and the Tamil community. After formally addressing them, I invited them to have tea with us, which was followed by a pleasant evening. Only then, I noticed a change of attitude in most of them. It would be safe to say that we were well on the path to reverting to the good old days of friendship and cordiality.

The next meeting that I organized was a good old rice and curry lunch for some of our British friends.

These meetings proved to be an immense success.

It served to prove to all Sri Lankans, living in the UK and elsewhere, that though various political decisions were made and implemented and though the official language policy segregated communities who had formerly lived together amicably, we could still live together in harmony and agreement, casting our dissimilarities aside. The staff of the High Commission and many of our well wishers were overjoyed at our considerable efforts of reconciliation. The crucial accomplishment of these meetings, which was mainly a strong sense of unity amongst the different racial groups, continued throughout my period in England. I accepted that various organizations had their differences and did exercise their communal feelings but it was understood that this prevailed at all levels. The only manner in which to deal with such situations was to be tactful, careful and mostly diplomatic in order to bring all communities together in agreement.

Not content to meet the Sri Lankan community only in London, I proceeded to work out a detailed programme so as to visit the north and meet fellow Sri Lankans living in Manchester and Scotland. Just before my visit, the Government in Sri Lanka changed once again. A new President was appointed – President Chandrika Kumaratunga, heralding a new era in Sri Lanka (see also annexure I).

The events that followed were brief and informal. I was promptly recalled, having being given 30 days to return. My plans went through an abrupt change – I barely had enough time to say goodbye to the many people I had befriended during my one and half years in London. I packed my bags and prepared to return home. Protocol demanded that any diplomatic representative before leaving had to call on the Queen on departure, which we did. She was gracious enough to present us with a photograph of us with her and the Duke of Edinburgh, which was autographed by both of them.

On my return, I met the newly appointed Foreign Minister, the late Lakshman Kadirgamar, who I always maintained, was in every sense a thorough gentleman. I had known him from my school days in Kandy, as he had beaten me in the 120 yards hurdles at a Central Province group meeting. He admitted that he himself had been unhappy with the abruptness of my recall and proceeded to rationalize the nature of politics and what individuals even remotely involved have to go through. What I then realized was how erratic politics can be. I had spent nearly two years on two of the best diplomatic assignments a High Commissioner could hope for – the outcome of appointments made and changed by three Presidents of my country.

But this time, I decided, that I was home for good.

Do Unto Others....

As presumptuous as it may seem, I believe that before I conclude, I need to talk of the welfare activities I got actively involved in, the funds that I founded which turned out to be an immeasurable source of satisfaction to many and myself.

Sri Lanka Army Benevolent Fund

After a discussion amongst officers at Gurunagar, during a few hours which we were relatively free, a discussion followed about the future of the next of kin of the officers in the army, in case of the death of a servicemen.

We came to a decision that a proposal should be written in order for payment to be continued in case of any emergency, to the families of the servicemen until one is 55 years of age; which is the age of retirement for a soldier. As requested, this proposal was handed over to the President who immediately granted cabinet approval to the idea. This proposal, as it was a morale booster, was not even prevalent in most developed countries.

The soldier today is allocated a better pay and given a wide range of allowances. The living conditions, medical services and facilities provided to the soldier have also improved considerably in spite of the increasing numbers in the armed forces. Medical facilities provided for the immediate family include pre-natal and maternity care.

The soldiers wounded in action have a modern well-equipped Military Hospital located in Ragama, which provides rehabilitation and after care services while also striving to find accommodation for the retired soldiers to live in dignity.

However, soldiers have to meet numerous demands and social obligations which require financial resources that have to be met when they are needed, as planning for it becomes virtually impossible whilst serving in operational areas. But urgent financial needs require urgent solutions which are not readily available from institutions in the public or private sector.

Previously, the army had to provide a soldier with three or four beds – one in the home station, perhaps two in the operational area and one in the hospital. This situation changed after the commencement of hostilities since the mid 1980s, and has not improved since. A soldier certainly has a permanent regimental 'home' base but he is often deployed to answer the call of duty which could mean spending years in the operational areas of the north and east. The result of this deployment is the lack of opportunity to indulge in any other work of any other nature.

To meet the routine demands of the day, it was obligatory for the Regiments/Battalions to provide financial relief to soldiers in distress and cater to urgent needs such as the payment of medical bills for the next of kin, a death in the family, religious obligations and other exigencies. At that time the pay and allowance given to soldiers was minimal and was definitely not enough to generate financial resources of any kind. Thus, there existed an urgent need to establish a 'savings' scheme with regard to the future financial stability and welfare of the soldier. The soldier did enjoy a gratuity but it did not commensurate with his service as a soldier at the end of 22 years, which is the period of service for a soldier. Most soldiers at the point of retirement were just over 40 years and most often rather 'young' to be without any means of employment or a steady source of income. Retirement, incidentally, is the time when the retired soldier or officer requires financial investment to educate his children and fulfil the growing social obligations. The lack of opportunity for a retired soldier meant that many of them faced a huge dilemma. This dilemma, I figured, could be resolved only with a well managed and attractive savings scheme approved by the army for which the soldiers could contribute whilst in service.

The army was obliged to provide financial assistance to help the retired soldiers begin a new venture in order to sustain themselves and the demands of their relatively 'young' families. The soldier was provided with a pension in the mid 1960s, which was in my opinion inadequate. There was also nothing more for the officers on the eve of retirement except the benefit of a gratuity and later a pension.

A retired soldier or officer most often could not engage in any other form of business which would generate extra finances. Many servicemen on retirement needed extra finances to provide for higher studies or to build a house of his own for his family. Unfortunately, the Regimental/Battalion savings scheme could not meet this need due to the limited resources. The loans, if granted, most often were on the basis of urgency.

As Commander, Support Forces using members of my own staff: Major K.M.S. Perera, Capt. Parry Liyanage and Capt. Ranaweera, in Panagoda, we managed to establish a savings scheme for officers and soldiers with their affordable contributions.

The essential rule was to save what officers and soldiers could afford and the bottom line was not being over ambitious. At first, the scheme was restricted only for troops in the Support Forces – the Armed Corps, the Ceylon Light Infantry, Artillery, Field Engineers, Signals, Military Police, Works Services and the Pay and Records Branch.

It was no surprise that the scheme became extremely popular! Before long, there were requests from all Units to extend the scheme throughout the entire army. This was encouraging for us and we tried to make sure that all possibilities were explored to base the scheme on financial expertise.

After many feasibility studies and discussions at various levels, with the leading banking community and financial experts, a special Unit supervised by the Army Paymaster was established at Panagoda adjoining the Pay and Records Branch next to my headquarters. The scheme began with modest aspirations with servicemen, irrespective of rank contributing Rs. 30 monthly which was done in the form of an official pay deduction. The scheme also provided for extra contributions through increments of Rs. 10 or multiples of Rs. 10.

It was natural that at the outset the scheme was not taken seriously by the usual cynic... It was natural for soldiers, or rather, I suppose, anyone to question deductions from the monthly pay and this was evident even when the pension scheme was extended by the government to the military. Some soldiers at the time, including many officers, were hesitant and unwilling to contribute to the pension scheme and many did so only after much persuasion!

The benefits of the Savings Fund, once realized, became popular beyond expectations... Today it is with great pride that I speak of the giant strides made by this scheme just 25 years since its inception in 1981. At that point, it was called the Sri Lanka Army Provident Fund. It was renamed in 1996 as the Sri Lanka Army Benevolent Fund (SLABF). The Fund was formulated within a legal framework and was governed by a constitution and based in the Army Cantonment, Panagoda, Homagama. It is governed by a board of trustees which include the Deputy Chief of Staff as President and eight other Senior Army officers. The eligible grounds for membership is being a "serving member of the Regular/Volunteer Force of the army", and the minimum contribution is presently Rs. 100.

Today, many senior officers who joined the scheme since its very early days have collected an unbelievable sum of over Rs. 2 million in savings prior to retirement. It was not only officers who benefited from what is today the SLABF, but the families too. Thousands of soldiers of all ranks depend on the benefits of the scheme prior to and after retirement.

On my part, as I reflect here, I must admit that it was extremely satisfying to see a scheme which began as an idea, substantiated with modest means and aspirations in 1981, grow up to provide a service which today satisfies the needs of all servicemen with tremendous financial support in order for him or her to live in confidence along with a definite sense of economic stability... The assets of the Benevolent Fund stand as at the end of 2005, at approximately Rs. 7,650 billion.

Project Thawalama

During my period of duties since the late 1970s and early 1980s as Commander Security Forces in Jaffna, I had the opportunity to travel mostly by road, as the benefit of a helicopter to supervise operations was rare during that time. The major requirement for operations did not involve many troops but were mostly from the three or four commando platoons under my command.

The Sinhalese as well as the Muslims who lived in the adjacent villages to those occupied by the Tamil people had lived in amity for many years. The villages of Yan Oya and Aththawetunu Wewa areas assumed greater importance to the Liberation Tigers of Tamil Eelam (LTTE) as they vigorously launched 'ethnic cleansing' to evict the Sinhalese and the Muslim communities from villages they considered a part of their 'Tamil Homeland' after the anti-Tamil riots in July 1983. It was after this incident that the LTTE started to claim, even more vociferously, that they were the "sole representatives of the Tamil people."

The LTTE began a well directed programme to drive away the Sinhalese from their ancient (*purana*) villages where they had lived for thousands of years. The method used was killing to instil fear and instability. This instilled fear and instability pushing them to isolation without food, as for generations agriculture was their only means of livelihood, which, without stability they could not practice. They were thus unable to maintain the irrigation channels that fed water into their paddy lands, which provided them with rice. The Yan Oya and Aththawetunu Wewa in the Weli Oya area not only served as a vital 'buffer zone' against the marauding LTTE from attacking other Sinhalese further south, but was also their staging and training area.

156

This area was the heartland of the ancient irrigation systems of the Sinhalese kings who ruled from Anuradhapura and Polonnaruwa.

I firmly believed that these villages needed to be rebuilt – to provide the villagers the basic needs, and this was most definitely a task for the government. It was around this time that I took the opportunity to assist and encourage Lieutenant Colonel Amerasekera to obtain his release from active service and involve himself fully in a task that was to provide those villages with their basic needs. He was able to instil confidence in the people, so as to bring them to work together, so that they may work at bringing a sense of order back into their lives.

After the first LTTE attack on those villages took place, more attacks were anticipated which resulted in a mass exodus of people to the south. Lieutenant Colonel Amarasekara began his project with the sole intention of preventing this and thereby organised 60 villages including those in the Yan Oya and Aththawetunu Wewa. The villagers wrote to me seeking support for the Thawalama project, as it was called, which was the result of his experience stemming from working as the Manpower Mobilization and Disaster Relief Coordinator for 2 Divisions. He had identified the affected villages as Padawiya, Sripura, Kebbitigollewa, Horowopathane and Gomarankadawela Divisional Secretariats in the Trincomalee and Anuradhapura Districts as being the main areas which face constant threat of LTTE attacks.

The 'Thawalama Project' helped the villagers regain their confidence and enabled them to live once again in their (*purana*) villages. The project helped maintain stability by not uprooting entire villages and moving them away without any direction to areas completely different in environment and agriculture compared to what they have been accustomed to.

Medical and Surgical Care for Armed Services Personnel

The Army Medical Corps has worked in spite of great difficulties to provide medical services for our troops in the field with some members of the Corps making the supreme sacrifice.

In my opinion, ever since the Unit was established, the Medical Corps has become today an inspiration and a critical morale raising factor for our troops. Providing medical support for all servicemen, their next of kin and even to extended families, the Medical Corps is mandatory in any army, providing the most critical service – the duty of relieving pain.

The soldier in the field ultimately answers the battle call, confident that he/she will be provided with the best medical facilities available in our country. The battle casualties of the IPKF did not fail to appreciate the dedication of our medical teams in the field. The Corps not only provided the essential medical services that were required but also became the vital factor in anticipating either success or failure with regard to operations, in order to maintain the morale of the troops at the highest levels.

"Ranaviru Sevena" was also established in the late 1989-1990 period, to provide care for the severely disabled. This facility was for the seriously injured servicemen needing special medical care. Numerous consultations had helped in deciding that the facility was to be in close proximity to a well equipped hospital. True enough, Colombo was considered too busy and crowded!

At that point in time, I was the General Officer Commanding and with the support of the Secretary Defence, General Sepala Attygalle, a specialist medical cover was organised for Special Operations troops in the north and east. The injured soldiers were to be treated first in the base camps in Palaly, Jaffna, and were then transferred to either Anuradhapura or Sri Jayewardenepura Hospitals where a special helipad was established.

Dr. Narendra Wijemanne, a surgeon attached to the National Hospital, Colombo, was one of the first to volunteer and treat casualties who were shifted to the Military Hospital, Colombo and the National Hospital Colombo, from the operational areas of Jaffna and the east. From what I recall, Dr Wijemanne offered his services and neither did he need much motivation by me or any other to lead medical teams to areas during operations. He saw the need and accepted the challenge in a manner which has to be duly commended. Special operations were repeatedly held in the Jaffna Peninsula: in Pallai, Elephant Pass, Kilinochchi, Mullaitivu, Parakaramapura, Mannar including Illupaikadavai, Uiyilankulam, Musali, Vavuniya and Trincomalee, which lasted two to about seven days at a time. These operations resulted in casualties – all essentials, the likes of dressing, drugs, disposable equipment for minor surgery, towels, drapes and intravenous fluids and blood were provided by the Army Hospital or by the Health Ministry. These items were packed and delivered by air to wherever they were required.

The Palaly Base Camp was clearly the biggest and the best equipped military hospital in the northern operational areas. The Commander of the Army at that time, Lieutenant General Nalin Seneviratne noticed the urgency of having a modernized and well-equipped medical facility in the operational area.

By 1985, the army had built a special medical facility in Palaly along with a large operating theatre, sterilizing room, a ward attached to the theatre which could be used as an intensive care unit and two large wards to accommodate a large number of injured troops. During large-scale operations there were two surgical teams. Most often the other medical officers were Dr. Lucky Dissanayake and Dr. Michael Abeyratne. Unfortunately in the early 1990s Dr. Lucky Dissanayake was drowned in the sea which was an irreparable loss.

It did not take long for me to realize that the armed Tamil separatists had to be eliminated sooner or later. The sooner the better, I thought. There was consensus to launch this operation first in the heart of the terrorists' stronghold and home ground, the Vadamarachchi area. It was to be the largest operation in every way. First, it involved a division plus troop's strength – three brigades plus the first in army history since independence. Secondly, this included the air force, the navy and the police as well as the civilian authorities. A Medical Corps officer was attached to each battalion moving with the forward troops. Immediate first aid was available in the battle area, and if required the injured soldier was evacuated by helicopter to the military medical facility in Palaly, where two medical teams were on standby to meet any eventuality. The commanding officers of the two leading Brigades, Brigadier Denzil Kobbekaduwa and Brigadier Vijaya Wimalaratne always emphasised the need to develop the existing medical facilities in Palaly prior to operations.

Medical Services for Civilians

The remoter areas of Sri Lanka became more isolated due to a variety of reasons: ranging from difficulty with regard to access, the risk of malaria, encephalitis, and worse, the fear of being killed by terrorists in the on-going crossfire. The JOC and the military at the time understood this urgent need for basic medical infrastructure but it was the prime responsibility of the government to provide it 'free' for every citizen.

The JOC along with field commanders, the likes of Brigadier Denzil Kobbekaduwa, Brigadier Vijaya Wimalaratne, Brigadier Lucky Wijeratne, the Coordinating Officers of Mannar, Trincomalee, Mullaitivu, Batticaloa, Vavuniya and Anuradhapura – realised that these facilities should not be limited only to the troops but also to the suffering civilians caught up in an armed conflict to which they had not in any way subscribed.

Many were the instances, especially in the Mannar sector where victims of snakebites, food poisoning, complicated pregnancies were airlifted to Anuradhapura Base Hospital due to the lack of an ambulance. Since strengthening the existing health care system would be a long term exercise which required huge financial resources, the urgency was to provide the people with mobile health services.

The health camps I visited with my wife were conducted frequently in many difficult areas in the Districts such as Mullaitivu, Mannar, Polonnaruwa, Anuradhapura, Trincomalee, Vavuniya, and Ampara

160

with medical personnel who volunteered their services. Drs. Hiranthi and Narendra Wijemanne were the pioneers who organised this project, whilst coordinating with the Ministry of Health to obtain drugs, dressings and other necessary requirements. The surgeons, physicians, and the rest of the dedicated officers made these camps popular and meaningful in spite of the numerous difficulties they endured, as I recall. There were also volunteers from "Sathsarana" to help in the organizational work so as to release the medical staff to attend to the more pressing needs of the sick.

Society (for) Advancement, Reconstruction, Development Activities (SARDA)

I would like to digress briefly before explaining the role of SARDA... My work as Chairman of this NGO started as early as the mid 1990s. It was largely influenced by my experience as a platoon commander in the early 1950s, as a 'young' officer in Diyatalawa.

I have always wondered why I always possessed this immense fascination for agriculture! I still wonder why – but the only viable reason that I could surmise was maybe because I saw my father practicing it. He too loved planting trees, as did many people of his generation. I felt that they planted trees even in their old age, so as to leave them for their children and the future generations.

My contribution was made first at the Army Recruit Training Depot (ARTD), Diyatalawa, where I first tried my hand at planting trees. I had the same opportunity when I was the Commandant of the Army Training Centre (ATC) as well as Garrison Commander, in Diyatalawa. With the advice and encouragement from an enthusiastic group of officers from the reforestation project based near the abandoned British old race course at Haldumulla, Beragala, a total of 4,000 acres of bare army land, including the army firing range area, Engineer Hill, Fox Hill, 'One Tree Hill' were chosen as tree-planting sites. The plants were obtained from the Forest Department in Haputale.

This area has now been transformed into the very picturesque Motor Cross course with an improved firing range providing facilities up to over 1,000 yards and field firing range for heavier weapons. The platoons were given hundreds of turpentine and cypress trees, which were to be planted along the beautiful roads in the vast rolling expanses of the ATC to add beauty to the already picturesque area.

During the days when petrol driven vehicles were widely used, the Kadugannawa Pass was irresistible... Passers by or anyone travelling by automobile from Colombo to Kandy always made a brief stop to allow the engines to cool off and view the Bible Rock before they climbed up the Kadugannawa Pass. It was quite common for the best vehicle to take at least three hours to get to this location from Colombo. As a result of almost every vehicle having to make a stop at this particular point along the journey, a number of small boutiques started propping up! First it was the occasional tea stop! Soon afterwards, many wayside stalls started appearing which sold not only tea but king coconuts, fruits and many types of sweetmeats. The stalls were indeed a refreshing way to while away the time spent there. But in my opinion, the stalls were a menace – the beautiful view was completely lost.

A few of the owners of the vehicles took the opportunity to get their cars washed besides the small waterfalls by the road. This was tolerable too but the next problem came to be the empty king coconut shells that were being thrown on either side of the road creating huge piles of garbage, which was not only an ugly sight to behold but more of a health hazard. When water was filled in these 'empties,' it attracted mosquitoes and other vermin. Instead of being the beautiful and breathtaking sight that overlooked the Pass, what it did was present the most unsightly scenario. It had become a garbage dump used by local as well as foreigners on their drive to or from Kandy. It was at the height of this problem that I felt that this had to be stopped!

There was also the devastation caused to the jungle, which not only spoilt the beauty of the area but also threatened the mountain wall, with landslides becoming a frequent occurrence blocking traffic for hours or sometimes for a few days.

To prevent this practice and more so to preserve the sight on this stretch of the road, I realized that it would not be successful or practical to introduce a ban on the sale of goods, or the construction of wayside stalls on the side of the mountain wall. The sale of young coconuts and king coconuts, cigarettes, soft drinks and sweets to visitors was turning out to be a lucrative business for the vendors and I could never have induced them to give up. It was then I realized that I had to provide an alternative location for business: the same one they were engaged in, but most preferably at the same time keeping the road clean and tidy.

The first step I figured was to win the goodwill and also the cooperation of the people engaging in the business involved there, without resorting to political favour of any sort. However, I did face a dilemma. But who was I to work with, in relation to the above problem? It was this need or vacuum that was filled by SARDA. Incidentally, I was elected President of SARDA at the very first meeting!

What is SARDA? SARDA is a voluntary organisation based in Mawanella, which is totally committed to rehabilitation and protecting the environment since 1997. The members are drawn from all walks of life and membership is open to anyone who is interested and willing to work in any capacity to improve the environment which is severely threatened through all types of pollution. How we went about this problem was interesting... We first constructed accommodation and settled the shop owners on the landside in more modern stalls which would blend easily with the environment, so that, as always, the visitors can refresh themselves. Fruit stalls obstructing the view of Devanagala, Bible Rock were removed and this opened up the view of the vast stretch of terraced paddy fields and the open country.

This NGO had one primary aim – to restore the status quo of the Kadugannawa Pass to its former pristine beauty by rehabilitating the environment that had been devastated throughout the years.

We also wanted to concentrate on the re-forestation of large tracts of land bordering the main highway known as the A-1 Route and the Colombo–Kandy railway track which snaked its way to Kadugannawa at a higher level to the road, compared to most places. This area had been completely denuded of trees as a result of the illicit felling for timber and firewood. Over 262,000 of the targeted 700,000 trees were planted on either side of the Kandy-Colombo Road (A-1) and along the railway line from Balana to Kadugannawa. Some of these plants are now over 10-feet tall while the slow growers are still hidden below the tall grass, which grows profusely! The tall grass, whilst preventing erosion, has the disadvantage of being   susceptible to manmade and natural fires that occur from time to time. In one instance over 50,000 trees that had been planted by SARDA were lost due to these forest fires and were later re-planted.

As members of SARDA, we commenced our ambitious project of reforestation and started supporting the local entrepreneurs to develop their small industrial projects from locally grown produce. The organisation has effectively replanted and reforested the catchments area of the Hingul Oya and the Ma Oya in the Kadugannawa–Balana area.

Over 22 varieties of useful endemic trees such as jak, mango, and avocado have been planted in the forest reserve and adjoining lands with the consent of the absentee land owners. These trees would help enhance and supply a more nutritious diet for maybe not everyone, but for most people, whilst at the same time being a source of excellent timber in the near future.

Thus, a main programme that was initiated by SARDA is the effort to popularise the growing of jak trees, which can sometimes be seen amongst the mixed vegetation, sometimes grown in government forest reserves or often through natural dispersal. The Englishman Robert Knox during his captivity in the Kandyan Kingdom, in the 16th Century, often spoke of the jak tree and its uses to man as mentioned in his book. In the Indian state of Mysore, there exists an experimental station for the development of jak, as a source of nutritious food and also to provide high quality timber. The Jak Development Foundation has a target, which is to plant nearly 2 million trees within the next few years. SARDA is affiliated to this project with the centre Weerya Seva Sansadaya being located at Werallepotha, Rambukkana. The centre is ambitiously involved in bud grafting, seed distribution and providing information about growing jak, the benefits of it and how to make it a source of self employment. The centre also processes jak in a variety of ways so that it can be exported to other countries mainly to the Middle East, since over one million Sri Lankans reside there for work reasons. Currently, we are in the process of modernising this venture, which I believe has immense potential. We also engage in planting selected flowering trees on either side of the A-1 Road from Mawanella to Kadugannawa, which is approximately a rough distance of six miles. Educating schoolchildren with regard to the importance of maintaining a healthy and clean environment and interacting with them in order to improve the natural surroundings of their homes and schools, while respecting animal and plant life, also became another pressing project.

The advantages of Effective Micro-organisms (EM) with regard to agriculture were introduced to the people of the near vicinity. Field trials were conducted in their own paddy lands one year prior to introducing this to the farming community. What was shown practically to them was that EM is not only an inexpensive method but also an environmental friendly one.

Our greatest achievement today is the development of the Kurulu Kele project which adjoins the Kegalle Town. This site has already been declared a nature reserve as it is a storehouse of old flora. The giant creeper, *Puswela* – Entada confertiflorous is one plant that can be found here. However, its close proximity to the main town area of Kegalle with the growing demands for building space, means that the area is threatened perpetually with illegal encroachment from the burgeoning population demanding land.

Conclusion – My Military Diaries

Ever since my retirement as the General Officer Commanding (GOC) in the year 1991, my friends and colleagues have suggested that I not only record for posterity my memories, but write about my career in the army, which spanned over a period of two generations. This venture has certainly not been easy for me. The process of writing has been long and difficult: tedious at times: satisfying at times…

When I accepted the appointment of General Officer Commanding, JOC, I had no illusions that it was going to be easy. Many expected me to simply wipe out terrorism. I took on the job with hope and fear. But being the GOC was for me a lonely assignment – where decisions had to be made for which I was solely responsible. I did not intend to pass the 'buck' to anyone. I always believed that the responsibility lay with me, and ONLY me. Thus although, I do not claim that I did anything special, there may be experiences recounted in the 'diary' of mine which might and ought to help future officers in conducting operations against the terrorists. The LTTE cannot be compared to the terrorists in British Malaya. The LTTE has international links which terrorists in Malaya never had – this factor is of the utmost importance.

It is quite natural that there are a few who have been my critics. It is even more natural that there will be even more with the reading of this memoir of sorts… But most of these critics, I can confidently say would have worked with me at some point. They would have served with me or under me. I regret very much that they did not endeavour to correct me then being critical is acceptable but criticism after nearly two decades, since I relinquished duties as an officer cannot be helpful to the service, to me, or for that matter, anyone else.

There has been much criticism in the western press about not letting their reporters into the battle areas of the recent operations against the LTTE. Those journalists who say who want to go into these zones are the first to cry help when things go wrong though they show much bravado. The London Times correspondent who sneaked into the LTTE area and who was injured is one example of what could happen in a conflict zone.

But there are also some journalists who create more problems than answers. One example is a reporter called Charulatha who got many stories out of the mouths of officers. There was one senior officer who was quoted by her as saying that the Army was tired after 20 years of fighting. Significantly, a few days after the statement was published the LTTE launched a major attack. If we say we can't defeat terrorism there is not much point in fighting a war.

A reason which I think finally made me write or commence writing was when I was told that failing to do so would mean that I have failed in my duties to record events that I had the privilege to witness. I was witness to not one event, but a series of events which made Sri Lanka the country it is today. It is in that spirit that I make this contribution.

At the same time I greatly appreciate the efforts of each and every one: officers, soldiers, friends and well-wishers who supported me often beyond the call of duty in many instances despite grave risks to themselves. Without their support, including their blood, sweat, toil and tears, whatever little I may have contributed, would not have been possible.

A question that is frequently asked from me today is why terrorism could not be defeated in its infancy in Sri Lanka. It would be unfair by me to sit here in my old age and give a single reason. But if one single reason is of vital importance, it would be that the international community had not yet come to accept the dangers of terrorism to the world, in the face of world peace. This single factor has made terrorist financing, propaganda, money laundering, arms smuggling, organizational networks a matter of grave concern to the international community which was not available back then. Countries today have listed terrorist organizations including the LTTE, which has now been accepted as one, if not the most dangerous terrorist outfit with international ramifications. This was also only after the assassination of Indian Prime Minister Rajiv Gandhi who was brutally killed by the LTTE. Other countries only went on to list the LTTE as a terrorist organization after 9/11. It was only since then that they have eased on the sale of weapons, rockets, ammunition and military hardware including aircraft to Sri Lanka. It is only now that India is totally supportive of the eradication of the terrorism unleashed by the LTTE. Many states have realized the vital importance of eliminating terrorism, the one single-most important factor threatening the world today. In my view, the world now is in a better position to eliminate terrorism than it was back then when I was in a place of power to take effective action.

Today as I write the LTTE has been defeated. But it will not be the end of Tamil militancy. STRATFOR, the US strategic security organisation, said in early 2009, 'The Tigers use India in much the same way that the Taliban and Al Qaeda use Pakistan. The Tigers' logistical and training infrastructure in India is especially important during times (like the present) when the Sri Lankan government is defeating them.' Despite pressure from Tamil Nadu, India is in a difficult position as China and Russia are on Sri Lanka's side. There are fears that China by developing the Hambantota Port will have a strategic advantage in the future, while Pakistan's relationship with Sri Lanka is also worrying India. Meanwhile the Indians are being blamed for the crisis in Nepal, while in Pakistan there have been accusations that Indians were involved in the attack on our cricketers in Lahore. Pakistan's fight against the Taliban in the Swat Walley at the insistence of America has led to humanitarian crisis with upto a million civilians involved. South Asia is in turmoil, but I hope Sri Lanka will enjoy more peaceful times in the future.

Genocide is a term that has been bandied about since the 1983 July riots but what is the word one can use to describe the killing of so many Tamils by the LTTE including their own leaders? Even at the time of writing the LTTE is holding a large number of civilians hostage and there are reports of them shooting those who are trying to escape.

What I have gone through for my country is indeed not short, or sweet. I retired from the army, which at that time comprised around 20,000 security forces. I gave up the uniform in the rank of Brigadier. In 1983, I was appointed Chairman of Airport and Aviation Services, an appointment I was reluctant to give up when I was nominated the General Officer Commanding in the rank of General in the early part of 1986. I succeeded the first GOC General T.I. "Bull" Weeratunga who was subsequently appointed the Ambassador to Canada.

It was a time when terrorism was gaining grounds with Tamil youth attracted to the ranks of terrorists by the unfortunate 1983 July anti-Tamil riots. At that time, the army comprised of relatively small numbers with enlistment steadily continuing. Back then, it was difficult to have a battalion in reserve. However, today there are three divisions in reserve. Even so, the threat perception, scale and intensity of fighting has also increased today, with the LTTE becoming more sophisticated. The security forces and the police have done excellently to keep the pressure on the LTTE. They have at the same time 'liberated' the Eastern Province to enable holding local elections without incident after 14 years. This certainly is an achievement.

One of the more satisfying experiences in my career was the planning and launching of 'Operation Liberation – One' in 1987. That was a generation ago. The operation was important for the simple reason that it was the first time that independent Sri Lanka was able to launch a division in the field against the opponent with support arms, the air force and the navy. The successful progress of 'Operation Liberation – One' could not be completed due to the Indian intervention and the events which followed. The experience however was important, not only for the armed forces and the police but also for the civilian administration and humanitarian staff and other agencies involved.

'Operation Liberation – One,' according to almost all reports was a critical point in the entire history of the war against terrorism. The Indian Peace Keeping Force took over our duties in the Northern and the Eastern Provinces while we were moved away to resolve the JVP insurgency in the south which intensified after the Indo-Lanka accord. The JVP saw the IPKF as India meddling in our affairs and perceived it as a threat to our sovereignty. It is with regret and sorrow I state here that if this intervention had not taken place, our war against terrorism would now be part of our history instead of being part of our present.

Destiny played a large role in my life. After decades of serving my country, after facing varied and dangerous situations, I am blessed to be able to sit here at my home in Mawanella and write these last few words. For me, my country is where my heart is. It can never lie elsewhere. I am still at home. At peace.

The long war against the LTTE has concluded. But that story is someone else's to tell…

ABBREVIATIONS

4D&C	4ᵗᵐ Development And Construction Engineers
AASSL	Airport And Aviation Services Sri Lanka
AGA	Assistant Government Agent
ANC	African National Congress
APC	Armoured Personnel Carrier
ARTD	Army Recruit Training Depot
ATC	Army Training Centre
CCC	Colombo Commercial Company
CID	Criminal Investigations Department
CIDA	Canadian International Development Agency
CJC	Criminal Justice Commission
CLI	Ceylon Light Infantry
CWC	Ceylon Workers Congress
CWP	Coast Watching Post
DDC	District Development Councils
DMK	Dravida Munnethra Kazagham
EM	Effective Micro-Organisms
EPRLF	Eelam Peoples Revolutionary Liberation Front
EROS	Eelam Revolutionary Organization of Students
FAO	Food And Agricultural Organization
FARELF	Far East Land Forces
FP	Federal Party
FSC	Ferret Scout Cars
GA	Government Agent
GOC	General Officer Commanding
GSO	General Staff Officer
GUES	General Union of Eelam Students
ICAO	International Civil Aviation Organization
IED	Improvised Explosive Device
IGP	Inspector General of Police
IPKF	Indian Peace Keeping Force
IRA	Irish Republication Army
ISD	Intelligence Services Department
JAC	Japan Airport Consultants
JOC	Joint Operation Command
JVP	Janatha Vimukthi Peramuna
KKS	Kankesanthurai
LRRP	Long Range Reconnaissance Patrol
LTTE	Liberation Tigers of Tamil Eelam

MGR	M.G. Ramachandran
MOD	Ministry of Defense
MP	Member of Parliament
NACO	Netherlands Airport Consultants
NCO	Non Commissioned Officers
NIB	National Intelligence Bureau
PLFP	Peoples Liberation Front Of Palestine
PLO	Palestine Liberation Organization
PLOTE	Peoples Liberation Organization Of Tamil Eelam
POL	Petrol And Oil Lubricants
POT	Potential Officer Training
PT	Physical Training
PWD	Public Works Department
QM	Quarter Master
RCDS	Royal College of Defence Studies
RMA	Royal Military Academy
RPG	Rocket Propelled Grenade
SARDA	Society (For) Advancement, Reconstruction, Development Activities
SF-HQ	Security Forces-Head Quarters
SF	Security Forces
SLABF	Sri Lanka Army Benevolent Fund
SLRC	Sri Lanka Rifle Corps
SLR	Self Loading Rifle
SP	Superintendent of Police
SSP	Senior Superintendent Of Police
TAFII	Task Force Illicit Immigration
TC	TAmil Congress
TEA	Tamil Eelam Army
TELA	Tamil Eelam Liberation Army
TELO	Tamil Eelam Liberation Organization
TULF	Tamil United Liberation Front
UN	United Nations
VIP	Very Important Person
VVT	Velvettiturai
WIP	Very Very Important Person
WO	Warrant Officers
ZANU	Zimbabwe African National Union
ZAPU	Zimbabwe African Peoples Union

INDEX

174

With my family

Communications with headquarters was not easy

Survivors of Intake 8 (1950-52) parade at the Royal Military Academy Sandhurst 50 years later

The shooting team

Inspecting the Guard of Honour in Canberra

1971 Insurrection in Kegalle

Patrolling in a Ferret Scout car during unrest in Colombo

Performing at the Army Tattoo at Sugathadasa Stadium

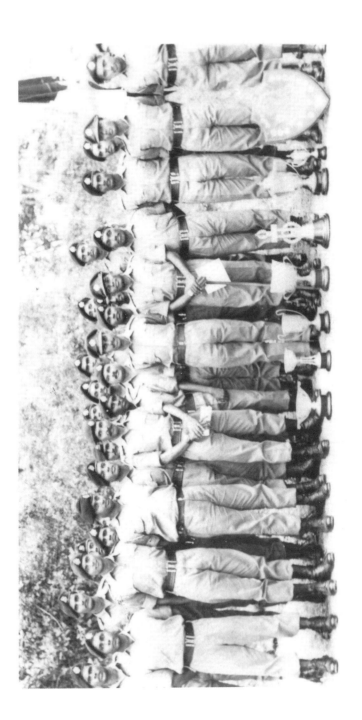

Inter Unit Rifle shooting Champions – 1st Recce Regiment

1971 Insurrection, Kegalle – Getting ready to fire

Damage done by the insurgents during the 1971 insurrection in Kegalle district

Our wedding day in London

On Board *Wilem Ruys* returning from London

Discussions with Indian Authorities during a visit to New Delhi

With Lt. Gen. Depinder Singh – Commander Indian forces in Sri Lanka

Prime Minister Mrs. Sirimavo Bandaranaike inspecting areas liberated from the JVP

Visiting 'tribes' during the African tour

With the Service Commanders in Jaffna

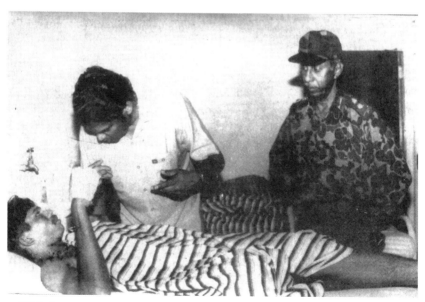

With the Minister Lalith Athulathmudali as he talks to an injured solider in a military hospital in Palaly.

Presenting credentials to the Governor of Australia

With the staff of the High Commission after presenting credentials

With the staff of the Sri Lankan High Commission in London

Meeting with Gen. Aslam Beg in Pakistan during a visit to Islamabad

Briefing the President of the intended battle plan

Commander Lucky Dissanayake

My son Rajind receiving the Vadamarachchi medal on my behalf from President
J.R. Jayewardene

At the opening of the new terminal building by President J.R. Jayewardene

General Sunderjee – Chief of Army Staff India, visiting me at the JOC headquarters

Meeting with Rajiv Gandhi when he arrived on the island to sign the Peace Accord

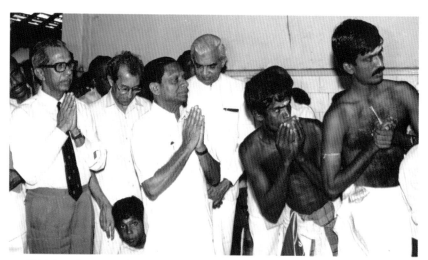

With President Premadasa, Bradman Weerakoon and Ranjan Wijeratne at a place of worship in the Northern Province

The author at the firing range

At JOC Headquarters after assuming office as General Office Commanding

Meeting with the President of Pakistan Gen. Zia Ul-haq at his residence

With Major. Gen.
Denzil Kobbekaduwa
and
Brigadier Wijaya
Wimalaratne during a
visit as
Defence Secretary to
the North

Meeting the Prime Minister of Japan at Katunayake

With President Premadasa after accepting the appointment as
Sri Lanka's High Commissioner in Australia

On my way to present credentials to Her Majesty the Queen

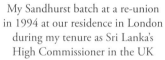

My Sandhurst batch at a re-union
in 1994 at our residence in London
during my tenure as Sri Lanka's
High Commissioner in the UK

Myrtle and I, with former
President of Nigeria, Gen. Jack
Gowon in U.K.

With General Sir Michael Rose in England

Environmental rehabilitation in Kadugannawa

Myrtle and Dr. Hiranthi Wijemanne distributing gifts among the servicemen

Now I am a farmer

My wife and I with our four grandchildren in Mawanella

My home.... in Mawanella